CONTENTS

INTRODUCTION   2

SCRIPT   3

SONGS
1. Have You Heard The Story?   12
2. Song Of The Trees   15
3. Who's That Knocking?   18
4. Check It Out!   21
5. Angel Conga   24
6. Listen To The News   28
7. The Children's Carol   32
8. Wise Men's Song   35
9. This Day   38
10. Baboushka (Reprise)   42

LYRICS   46

LICENCE DETAILS   56

© 2001 OUT OF THE ARK MUSIC

INTRODUCTION

There are many different versions of the tale of Baboushka, most of which involve Baboushka seeking the baby Jesus, but never finding him. In this version, however, her search is successful, giving hope to us all…

SETTING

Baboushka's house is set stage left, containing a table and chair and optional shelves/ornaments for Baboushka to polish. There is a lamp on the table. It may be useful to mark the position of the door on the floor. Upstage right, there is a large star (suspended), and a stable scene. This could be indicated by a silhouette cut-out of a crib, and/or by the actors themselves. Depending on available space and the number of children playing trees, they can be grouped between Baboushka's house and the stable and down stage of the stable.

CHARACTERS

Baboushka	*A stubborn, bad-tempered old woman**
Boris	*Her husband*
Tiddles	*Baboushka's cat*
Trees	
Chuck & Patti	*American tourists*
Popstar(s)	*Can be called something like* Eastern Spice/Eastlife
Bodyguard(s)	*to the above*
Children	*(1-4 have speaking parts)*
Mario & Antonio	*Pizza delivery men*
Beggar woman	
Shepherds	*(1-4 have speaking parts)*
Angels	*(1-4 have speaking parts)*
3 Wise Men	
Mary	
Joseph	

You may like to find an opportunity for some children to dance across the stage spreading 'stardust'.

*It should be possible for two reasonably similar children to share the part of Baboushka, the exchange taking place just prior to the entry of the angels.

BABOUSHKA

Baboushka is in her house, cleaning. The trees are in position and Tiddles is lying down among them.

Song 1 **HAVE YOU HEARD THE STORY?**

Tiddles	*(Moving to front of stage)* Hello, my name's Tiddles. I belong to that lady over there. Her name's Baboushka. She's actually not a bad old stick, though she can be <u>very</u> stubborn – but I can't complain, she gives me my pongy pilchards and stinky sardines every evening right on time.
Baboushka	*(Holding her nose)* Tiddles!
Tiddles	See!
Baboushka	Here kitty, kitty! *(Tiddles stretches and moves slowly across; but before Bab gives Tiddles the dinner she sees her husband coming and puts it on the table)* Ah! Here comes that good-for-nothing husband of mine. I hope he's got what I asked him for.
Boris	*(Sitting down at table)* Cartwheeling caterpillars, what a day! Well, at least I got all you wanted. It was very crowded at the market though – all the extra people for the census, I suppose. Every inn in town is full! Have <u>we</u> got any vacancies?

Tiddles is trying to reach dinner on the table and nearly gets it when…

Baboushka	*(Banging the table)* No we haven't! And if you think I'm going to try and make room for any more you've got another think coming! I've worked my fingers to the bone already! Do you know how many people have been up and down this road today, tramping through my garden? There's been chat…
Boris	*(Reeling off a list he's heard before)* …Chatterbox children, bawling babies, moaning mums, groaning grandads, shouting shepherds, dozy dogs…
Tiddles	Sounds just like the school gates at …………..! [*Fill in name of school*]
Baboushka	…<u>All</u> of them kicking up dust. I'll never get this house clean!
Boris	It always looks clean to me.
Baboushka	Well, it isn't! *(Boris sighs)* But it's nothing that some good old-fashioned housework won't sort out. *(She begins cleaning again)*
Boris	*(Looks out of the window)* My, my, that star is <u>so</u> bright – we don't even need to light the lamps!
Baboushka	*(Opening shopping)* What's this? This isn't what I asked for! *(Takes out can of coke and bag of crisps)*
Boris	Yes it is. Here, I've still got the list.

Baboushka	Don't try to confuse me with bits of paper! I know what I asked for and this is not it.
Boris	But look…*(He tries to show her the list, she walks away dusting)*
Baboushka	La, la, la!
Tiddles	*(Following Bab)* She always does that – starts to sing to herself when there's something she doesn't want to hear!
Boris	Whistling worms! You're such a stubborn old woman! I'm going out to the Crook and Fleece – to catch up on the news!
Baboushka	I don't know what you want to do that for. The only news we ever get around here is bad news! *(Boris exits. Bab thinks for a minute)* Oh Tiddles, I wish I could keep my mouth shut sometimes. I don't mean to be so horrid, but I think I'm just too old to change. I'm afraid there's no hope for someone like me! *(Goes about doing housework. Tiddles tries to reach dinner: just as he does, Baboushka moves bowl absentmindedly to clean)*

Song 2   SONG OF THE TREES

Baboushka	The wind is really whistling through the trees tonight, Tiddles. Maybe there's a storm on the way.

Throughout the next section, Tiddles keeps trying to reach his dinner and mimes getting increasingly weak and hungry without being too intrusive.

Enter Patti and Chuck: two loudly dressed American tourists.

Patti	Gee honey, this looks like a cute place, let's try here!
Chuck	Okay sugar, whatever you want, my little pumpkin!

They knock

Chuck	Hellooo! Anybody home?

Baboushka comes to the door

Chuck	*(Talking very loudly and slowly as if to a deaf person)* Hi there! We… would… like… a… room… for… tonight.
Patti	We thought your little cottage just looks good enough to eat! And with that liddle iddy biddy great big star right up there, it looks so romantic!
Chuck	It sure does, my little honey pie! It lights up the woods almost as much as you! *(Very loudly again)* So… have… you… got… a… room?
Baboushka	*(Very loudly and slowly)* No… I… haven't! *(Shuts door on them)*
Patti	Well, that's what you get for being nice to the locals! *(Exit towards stable)*

Enter Popstar(s) with bodyguard(s). There could be one or more – for example Eastern Spice *or* Eastlife.

Popstar	This place looks perfect. Just what I need to get away from the adoring crowds – and there's the brightest star I've ever seen right up there – it must be meant for me! *(Bodyguard knocks on door)*
Bodyguard	Open up! You'll never guess who I've got out here – Eastern Spice/Eastlife! It must be your lucky day, having someone that important come to stay!
Baboushka	*(From inside – holding nose)* Beeep! I'm sorry, there's no-one at home at the moment. Please leave a message after the tone. *(Blows very loud raspberry and resumes cleaning)*
Popstar	Well, really!

Bodyguard(s) gather round and tend to Popstar's ego. The entourage moves towards stable side to allow room for children. During this section Bab moves Tiddles' dish and is about to give it to him again just as children knock. Enter Children.

Child 1	*(Pointing in direction of* Eastern Spice/Eastlife*)* Hey! Look at that huge star over there. Let's go!
Popstar	*(To bodyguards)* I can't give any more autographs tonight! Send them away!

Bodyguard get ready to block kids who go right past and look up at the sky.

Child 2	I've never seen such a shiny star.
Child 3	Look! I bet this is stardust!
Child 2	The trees were right. They said this was a special night and it is.
Child 4	*(Miming picking up stardust)* Wow! This is so cool!
Child 1	*(Knocking on door)* Could we please have a jar to collect some stardust? It's fallen from that big star right there!
Baboushka	Stardust! All we've got here is plain ordinary dust and plenty of it! You've been eating too many blue smarties. Be off with you! *(Sweeps them away with her broom)*
Child 4	Come on! Let's just follow the trail.

Children exit, winding through trees. Enter pizza delivery men.

Popstar	It's getting so crowded here. *(Very dramatically)* Take me away, I want to be alone!

Exit – possibly through audience with bodyguard(s) saying 'No photos', 'No autographs', etc.

Pizza men knock.

Song 3   WHO'S THAT KNOCKING?

(During song pizza men play 'hot potato' with pizza. At end of song, they knock again. Bab opens door)

Baboushka	What is it now?
Mario	One-a marguerita with extra anchovies, tuna, prawns and more-a anchovies *(Italian accents if possible. During this section, Tiddles looks at first hopeful, then despondent in the background)*
Antonio	…And-a for-a dessert, justa one cornetto!
Baboushka	I didn't order any of this!
Mario	Boris and Baboushka's B and B. That'sa here, isn't it?
Baboushka	Yes, but I didn't order anything.
Antonio	You musta have done! Or maybe-a one of your guests!
Baboushka	Why would they order pizza when they've got my good home cooking? *(Pizza men shrug)*
Mario	Who'sa gonna pay for it?
Baboushka	If you hurry, there's a big crowd going that way. They mighta want to buy a slice!
Antonio	But it definitely says-a your address-a.
Baboushka	La, la, la, la. *(Starts dusting again)*
Tiddles	*(Making 'foiled again' sign)* There's no chance now! She'll never change her mind! Why does she have to be so stubborn?
Mario	Pizza, pizza, get your pizza here! Hey Antonio! Look at that-a star-a! I've-a never seen anythinga like it. It'sa even bigger than Pavarotti! *(They exit)*
Baboushka	*(Remaining in doorway)* What <u>is</u> going on tonight? There's certainly a funny feeling in the air. Tiddles… must be that storm… let's go and put our feet up for two minutes!

Enter beggar woman with baby.

Beggar	Can you spare a little milk for me and my baby?
Baboushka	Oh! Does it never end? Be off with you. I haven't got anything for you. *(They go and sit at side)*

Trees   Ba<u>oush</u>ka, Ba<u>oush</u>ka He calls you by <u>name.</u>
He <u>loves</u> you Baboushka and <u>for you</u> He came.

Baboushka   Who's there? Did someone say my name? *(Pauses)* Oh, I must be imagining things. Must be the wind rustling the trees again.

Shepherds run on. They are very out of breath and excited. Their words almost tumble out on top of each other.

Shepherd 1   You
Shepherd 2   just
Shepherd 3   won't
Together   believe it!

Shepherd 1   Angels
Shepherd 2   everywhere –
Shepherd 3   singing,
Shepherd 4   bright lights,
Together   absolutely fantastic!

Baboushka   What <u>are</u> you rambling on about?

Shepherd 4   The star… Look! *(They all jump up and down with excitement)*
Shepherd 1   We had to tell you –
Shepherd 2   As many people as possible!
Shepherd 3   And you're so close to the star!

Baboushka   Will you please tell me what you're on about? Have you been at the sheep dip or something?

Tiddles   Maybe they're just baaarking mad!

Shepherd 4   Just let us get our breath.

Song 4   **CHECK IT OUT!**

Shepherd 1   We're off now –
Shepherd 2   back to the stable –
Shepherd 4   to see the baby king!
Shepherd 3   Come with us!

Bab folds her arms and stays firmly put.

Shepherd 4   If you change your mind, follow the star! *(They begin to exit)*

Trees   *(Very quietly)* Baboushka! Baboushka!

Shepherd 4   *(Turning back)* See you! *(Baboushka trembles a bit)* Hey! You look a bit chilly.

Baboushka   It's just goosebumps!

Shepherd 1	Have this, it'll keep you nice and cosy! *(Gives Bab a fleece. They run off)*
Baboushka	What was that all about? I've never heard such a load of nonsense! Stars, angels, stables? They're not <u>fit</u> to be left alone with a flock of sheep! Woollyheads!
Trees	Good news, good news, sounds through the night. Good news for you and all of mankind, A baby is born, he is given this day, He calls you, Baboushka, please don't turn away! *(Repeat quietly under Babs' next speech)*
Baboushka	I'm hearing things! I need to get my ears waxed! *(She and Tiddles put their little fingers in their ears and wiggle them).* There's something very strange going on tonight! La, la, la.
Tiddles	If I don't get some food soon there'll be a cat-astrophe!

Enter a group of Angels chanting the following to conga rhythm.

Together	Oh, what a lovely evening, the brightest star is shining. A special night, a splendid sight!
Angel 1	Hello, Baboushka! Isn't it a wonderful evening? *(To others)* Almost there! Wow, just look at the shine on that star! *(Shouts up)* Well done, Gabriel! You've done a lovely polishing job. *(All wave upwards)*
Angel 2	Star light, star bright. There's good news to share tonight!

Song 5   **ANGEL CONGA**

During the first verse (instrumental) a group of cool angels dance onto the stage, moving in time with the music.

Angel 3	Hey, look, there's even stardust here! This is a real celebration!
Angel 4	Why don't you come with us, Baboushka? Come and see the baby!
Baboushka	Because <u>I'm</u> still right in the head! What would I want to see a baby for? Messy little things! And what's all this dancing and dressing up in silly costumes? You lot have been watching too much 'Stars in their eyes'!
Angel 1	Maybe you'll change your mind!
Baboushka	*(Putting hands firmly on hips)* This lady's not for turning!

Angels conga off, repeating chant.

Baboushka	*(Shouts after them)* Hey! How did you know my name?

Trees	A baby is born, he's given this day, He calls you, Baboushka, please don't turn away!
Baboushka	I think I'm going mad… *(She rubs her eyes)* Even those wings looked real. And I could swear the trees are whispering to me! It must be my age.

Song 6   **LISTEN TO THE NEWS**

Baboushka	You know, Tiddles, I really think there's something fishy going on over there. *(Pointing in direction of stable)*
Tiddles	I wish there was something fishy going on over <u>here</u>! *(Rubs his tummy)*
Baboushka	Oh, Tiddles! Your dinner! With all this nonsense going on, I almost forgot! Why didn't you say! *(Tiddles pulls 'what do you do with them' sort of face)*

Song 7   **THE CHILDREN'S CAROL**

The children gather around the stable scene, facing the audience. During song Bab gives Tiddles his dinner and strokes him.

Baboushka	Did you hear those children's voices carried on the wind? I'd forgotten how lovely children's singing can be. And what was that name they sang? Jesus? Almost made me want to cry. I must be getting soft in my old age. Pull yourself together, Baboushka! You've got work to do – a woman's work is never done!

Enter three Wise Men. Bow elaborately

Wise Man 1	Oh, Madam! Most Radiant Jewel of the Forest! Deepest apologies for troubling you on this magnificent evening. We are three weary Kings, in need of a glass of water, after our long journey in search of the Holy Baby.
Baboushka	Yes and I'm the Queen of Sheba. So where's the fancy dress party?
Wise Man 2	Oh Glorious Flower of Loveliness! We know you must be desperate to see the baby yourself and we do not desire to delay you, but our throats are as dry as the deserts we have crossed.
Wise Man 3	And we earnestly desire, O Ray of Sunshine, to sing out our praises to the King!
Baboushka	I suppose I can spare a little water – you could do with washing all that flowery nonsense out of your mouths! I don't know what you mean about this evening being magnificent. <u>Weird</u>, more like! And I'm <u>not</u> in a hurry to see any baby. There's one born every minute!
Wise Man 3	But not like this one, O Ruby of the East. This one's special. He's a Glorious King!
Baboushka	Then what's he doing being born out here? There are no private hospitals in this part of town! *(She goes and fetches water)*

Wise Man 1   *(Bowing)* You are so kind madam, Oh Eighth Wonder of the World!

Wise Man 2   *(Bowing)* We will be eternally grateful to you!

Wise Man 3   But now we must be on our way. Please accept this very small gift as a thank you. Farewell! *(Bows and gives Bab a candle. The Wise Men turn to look at the star)*

Song 8   **WISE MEN'S SONG**

At end of this song they bow again and exit.

Baboushka   I must be dreaming! I'll pinch myself and wake up. *(Pinches herself)* Ow! *(Smiling)* Jewel of the Forest, indeed! *(Looking at the fleece and candle)* People giving <u>me</u> gifts! Whatever's in the air tonight is going to my head. I almost feel young again – I feel quite giddy! Whatever next?

She sees the Beggar Woman, thinks for a moment then goes indoors and comes out with some gifts.

Baboushka   Here, have some bread and this shawl for your baby! I knitted it many years ago for a baby of my own, but sadly I've never needed it! *(Pause)* Anyway, here's some milk.

Beggar   Thank you, thank you! *(Hugs her)* You won't regret this!

Baboushka   Now, now! You'll break my old bones. *(Wipes a tear away and turns to star. Beggar woman exits).*
That star really is <u>very</u> bright. Maybe there is something special going on. Perhaps for once I'll leave the housework and go and see. *(She decides)* Yes! We could go together. Oh, where's she gone? Never mind, I'll have to go alone.

Trees   Baboushka, your heart has softened for sure,
Now joy will come in through love's open door!

Mary and Joseph and others come forward as Baboushka mimes going to the stable.

Trees   This baby was born in a stable so bare,
But love, joy and majesty lay with him there.
There's always a welcome for young and for old;
A gift of pure love, much more precious than gold.

Boris   Baboushka!

Baboushka   Boris! What are you doing here?

Boris   It seems there really is some good news tonight for a change – I didn't want to miss it! I'm really glad you're here, too!

Baboushka	*(Sees angels, who wave, and shepherds)* So it's all true! And it seems like the whole world knows about it. Isn't that ....? [*Insert name of famous footballer/rugby player/athlete*]
Children	Yeah!
Child 1	And look! There's our teacher with the Prime Minister!
Baboushka	Oh Boris! It's so exciting!

Wise Men and Shepherds give their gifts.

Wise Man 1	To the most precious of gifts, I bring Gold.
Wise Man 2	To the one who brings the fragrance of joy to the world, I give Frankincense.
Wise Man 3	To He who adds true flavour to life, I bring Myrrh.
Baboushka	Oh! Don't they speak beautifully? What can I give? Everyone has been so kind to me. *(Looks at gifts she's been given)* Perhaps I could give these… *(Laying down her gifts)* What a beautiful baby!
Mary	They look just perfect. A shepherd's fleece… for the good shepherd!
Joseph	And a candle for the light of the world!
Boris	Slithering snakes, Baboushka! What a night!
Baboushka	You're right, Boris. To think I almost missed it. I think there's something I ought to say.
Boris	You don't have to say anything.
Baboushka	Oh yes, I do!
Boris	*(Smiling)* Stubborn old woman!
Baboushka	Not any more. I think I've learnt my lesson!
Song 9	**THIS DAY**
Tiddles	I just love happy endings – and a full tummy – absolutely purrrfect!

At this point, Tiddles could stand with the pizza delivery men and share some pizza!

Song 10	**BABOUSHKA**

HAVE YOU HEARD THE STORY?

Words and Music
MARGARET CARPENTER

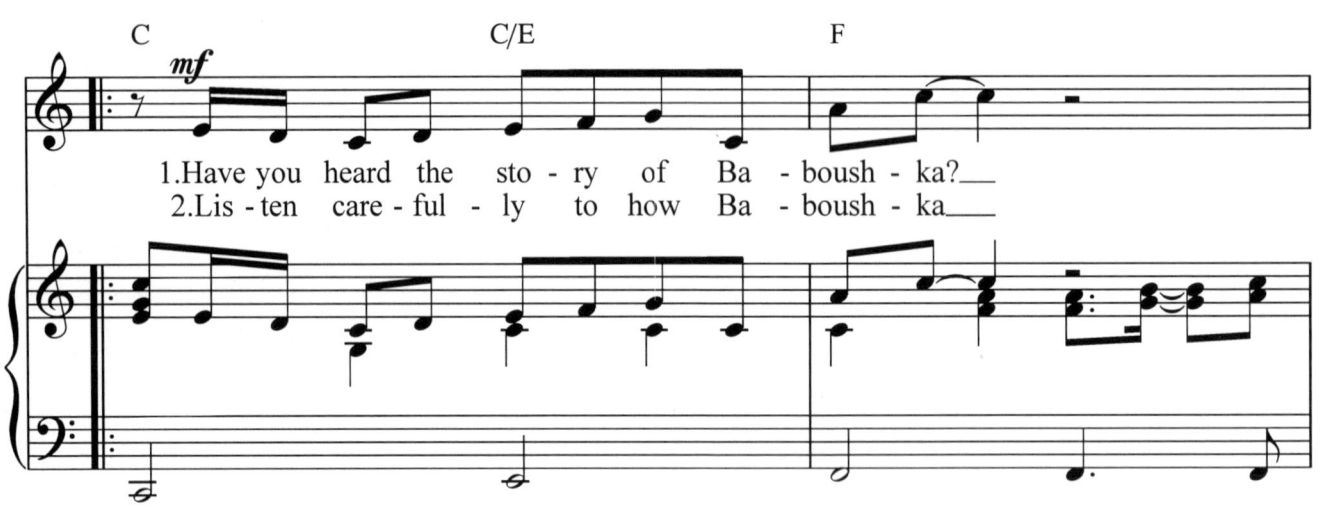

1. Have you heard the story of Ba-boush-ka?
2. Lis-ten care-ful-ly to how Ba-boush-ka

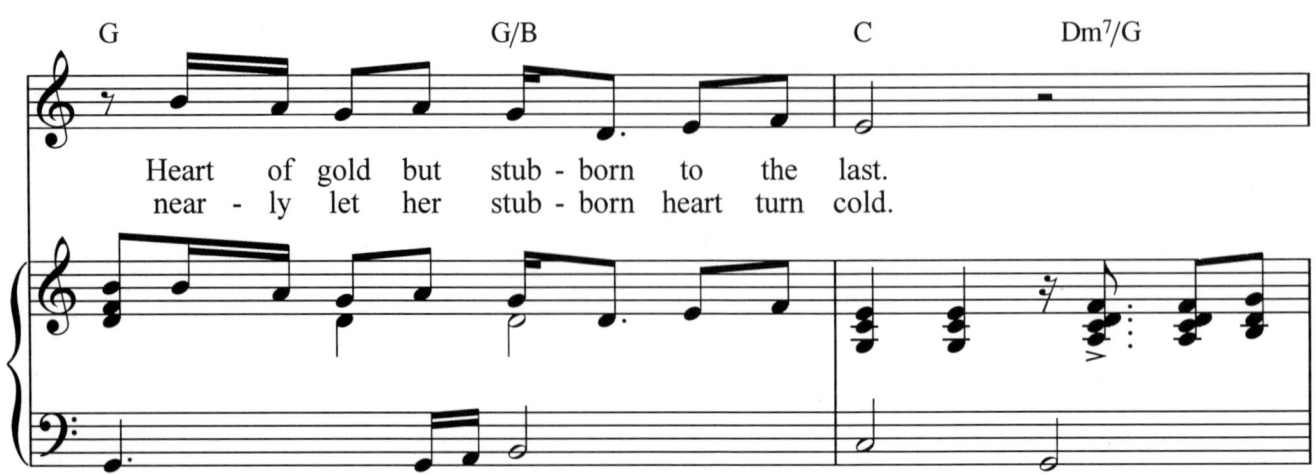

Heart of gold but stub-born to the last.
near-ly let her stub-born heart turn cold.

Copyright © 2001 OUT OF THE ARK MUSIC

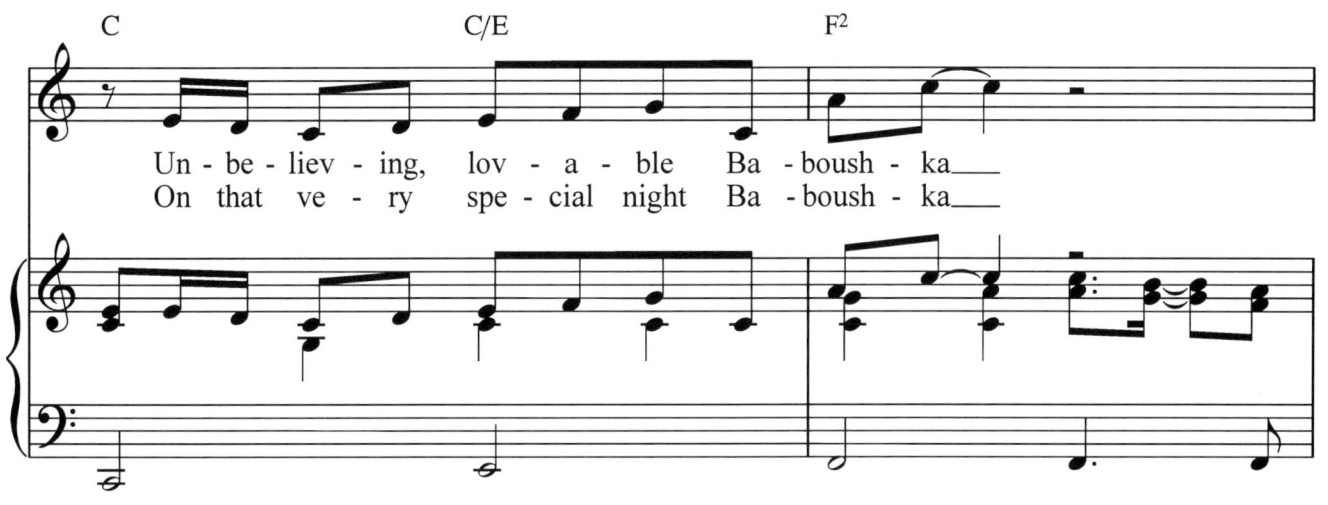
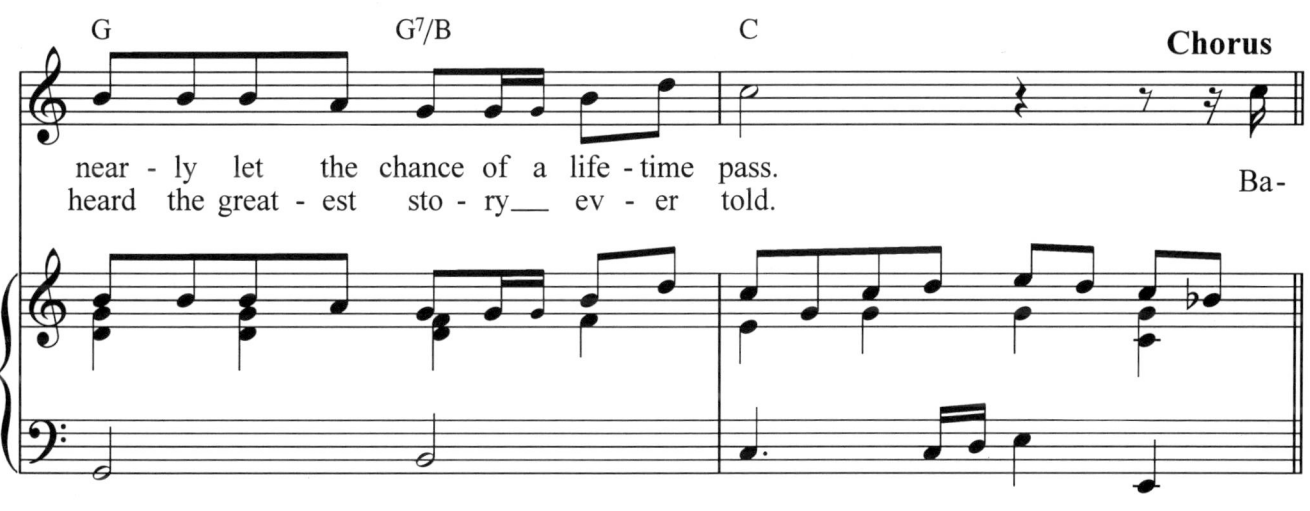

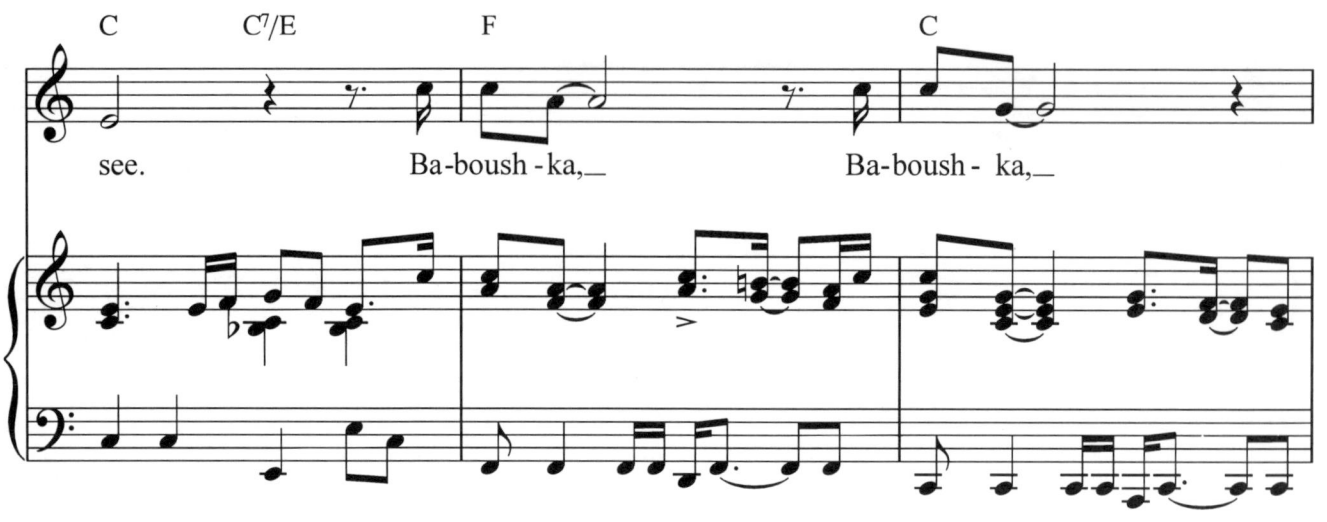

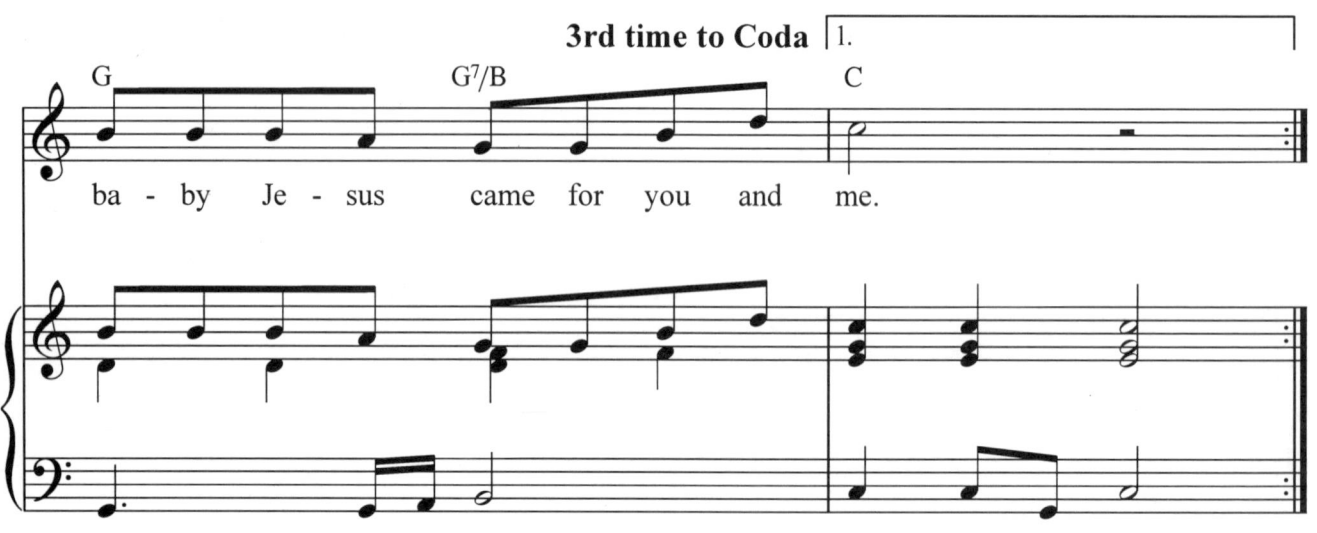

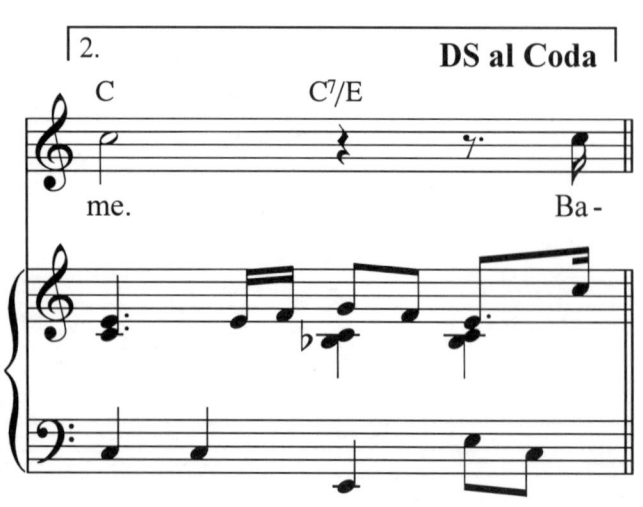

SONG OF THE TREES

Words and Music
MARGARET CARPENTER

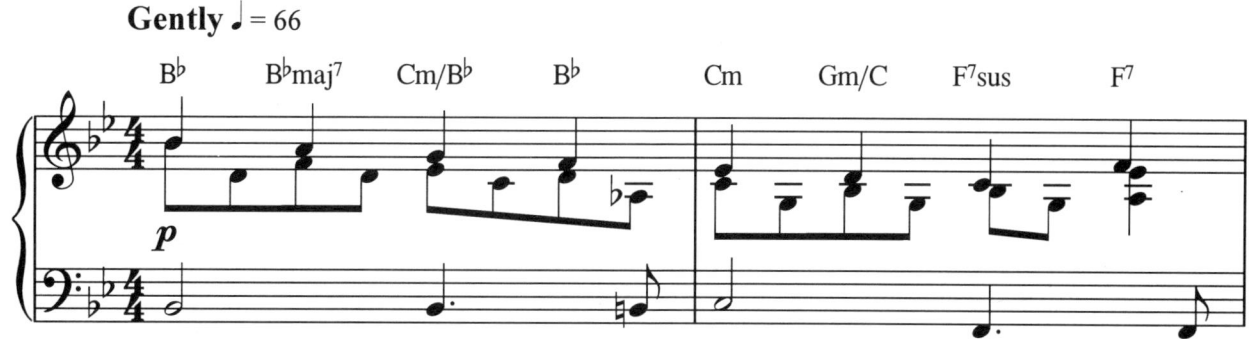
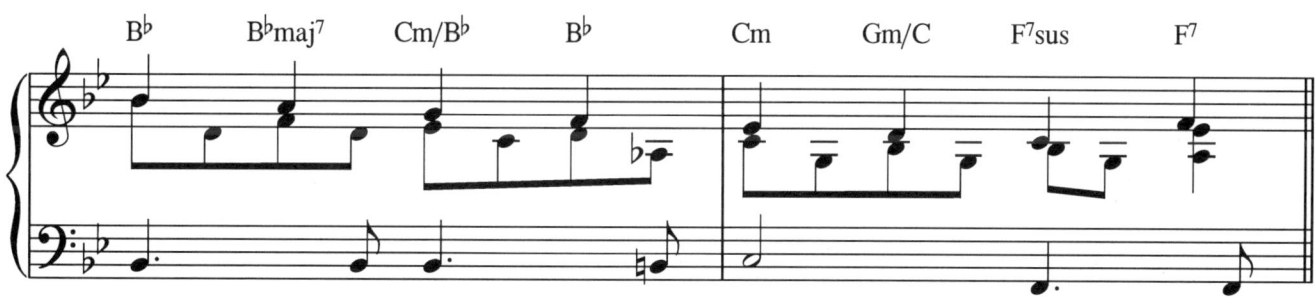
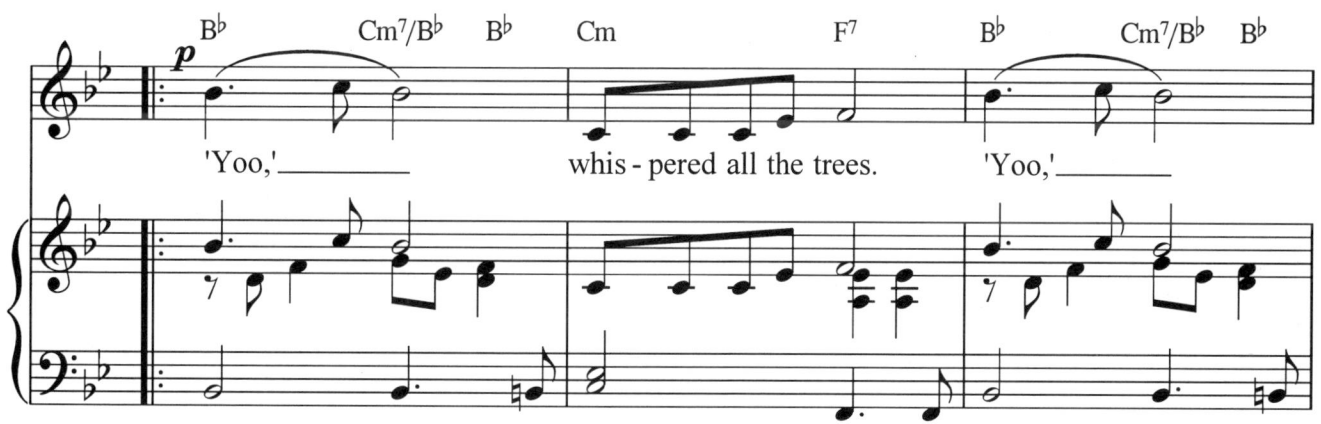

Copyright © 2001 OUT OF THE ARK MUSIC

17

WHO'S THAT KNOCKING?

Words and Music
MARGARET CARPENTER

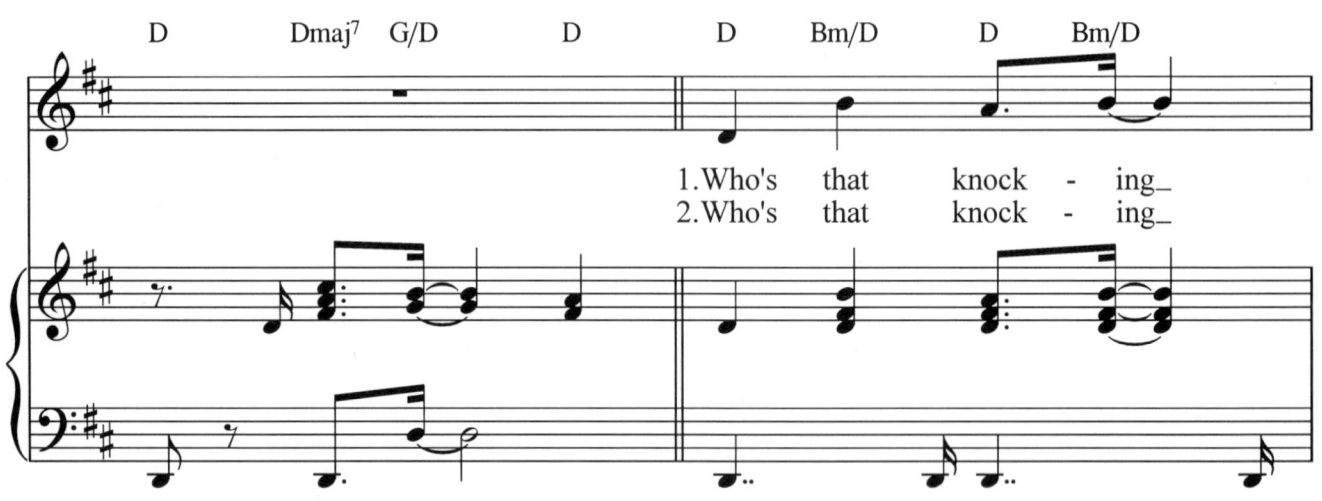

1. Who's that knock-ing on my door, can I ne-ver get a mo-ment's peace?
2. Who's that knock-ing on her door, can she ne-ver get a mo-ment's peace?

Copyright © 2001 OUT OF THE ARK MUSIC

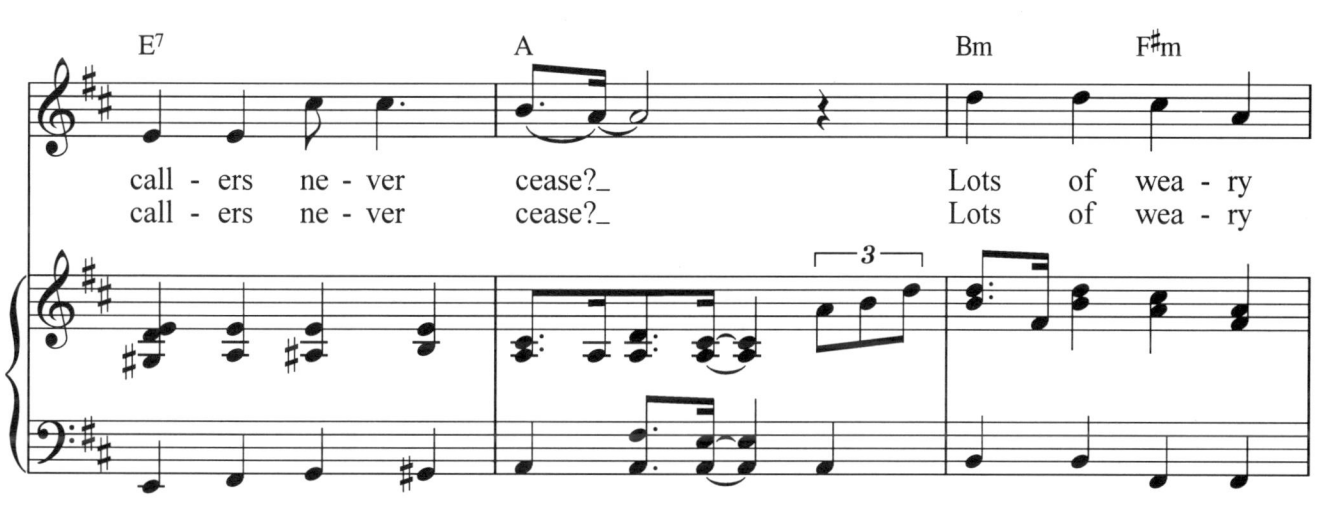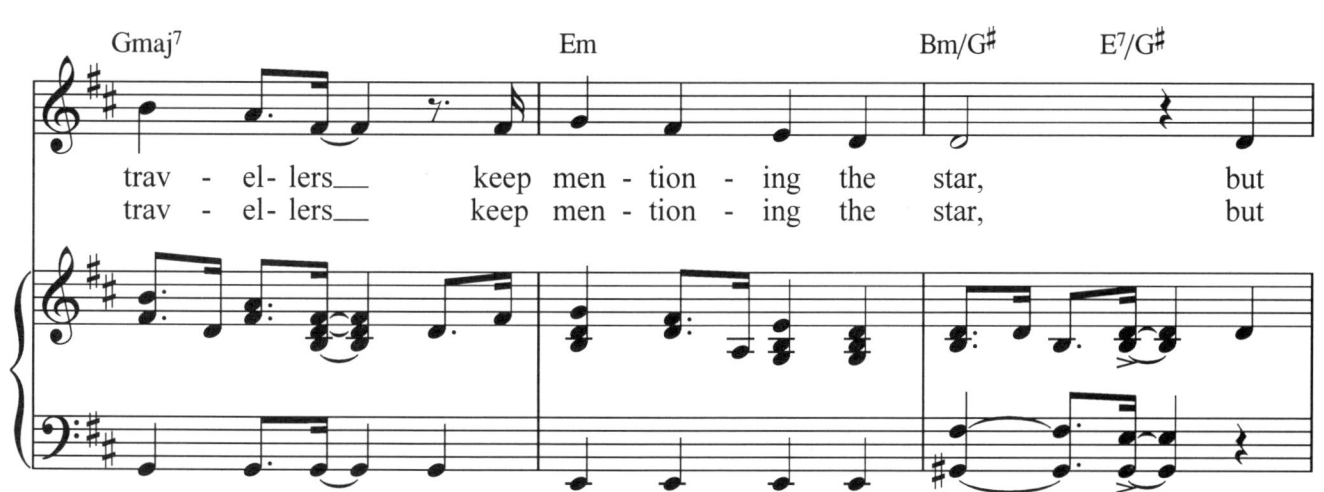

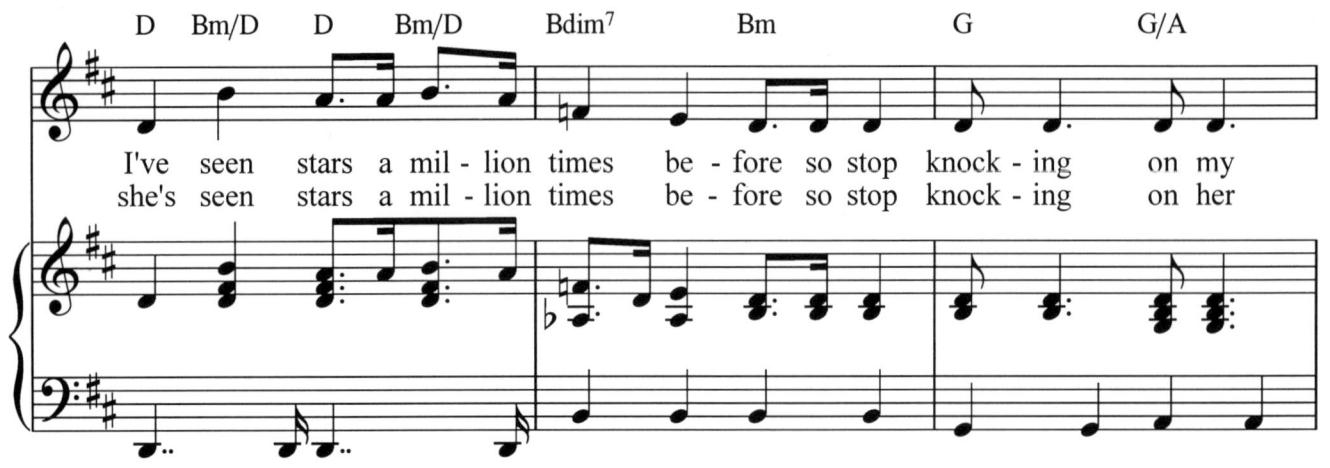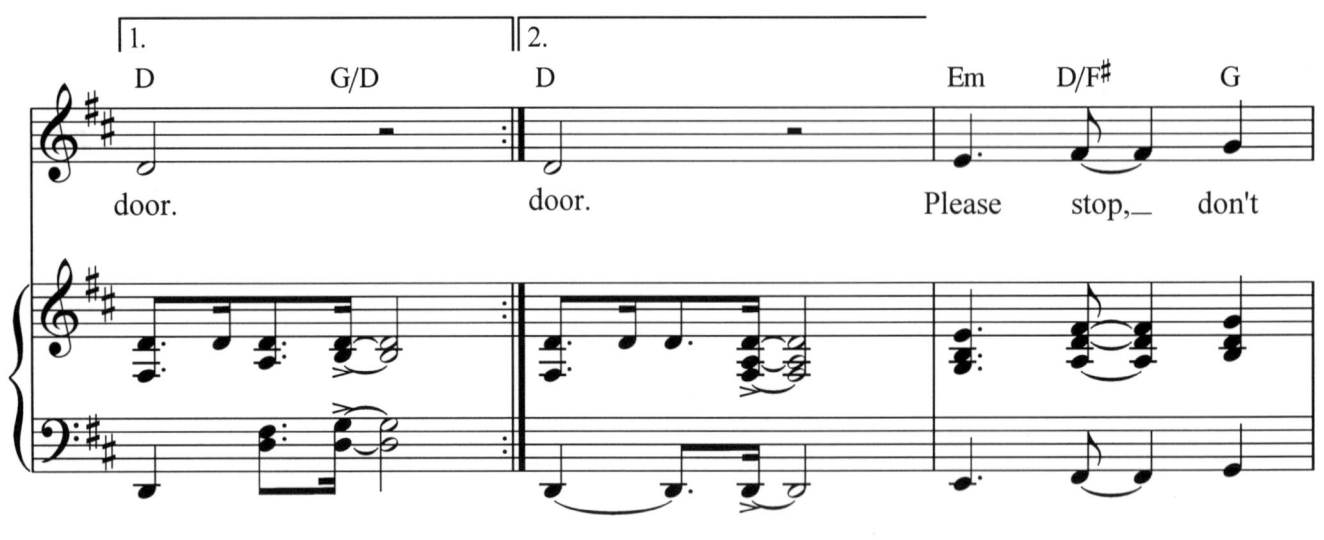

CHECK IT OUT!

Words and Music
MARGARET CARPENTER

In a reggae style ♩ = 88

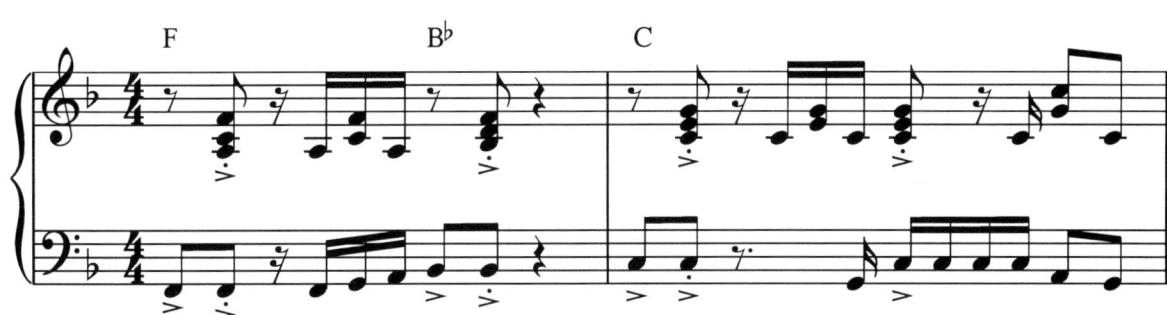

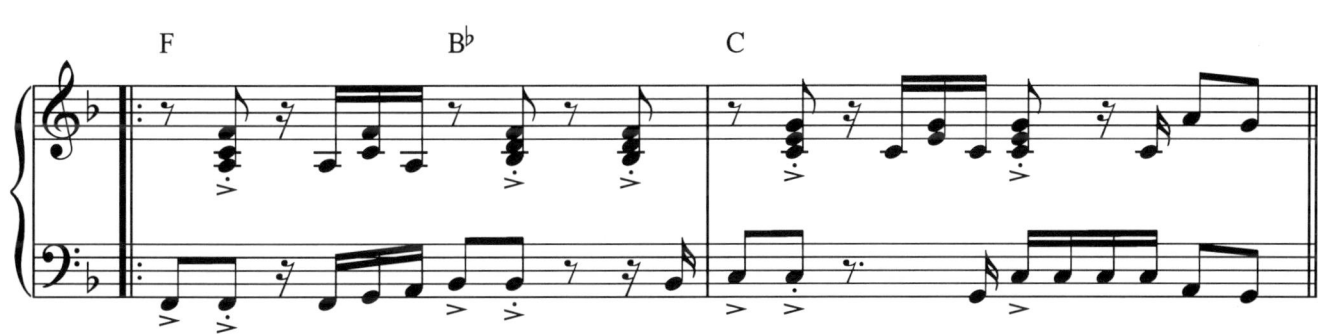

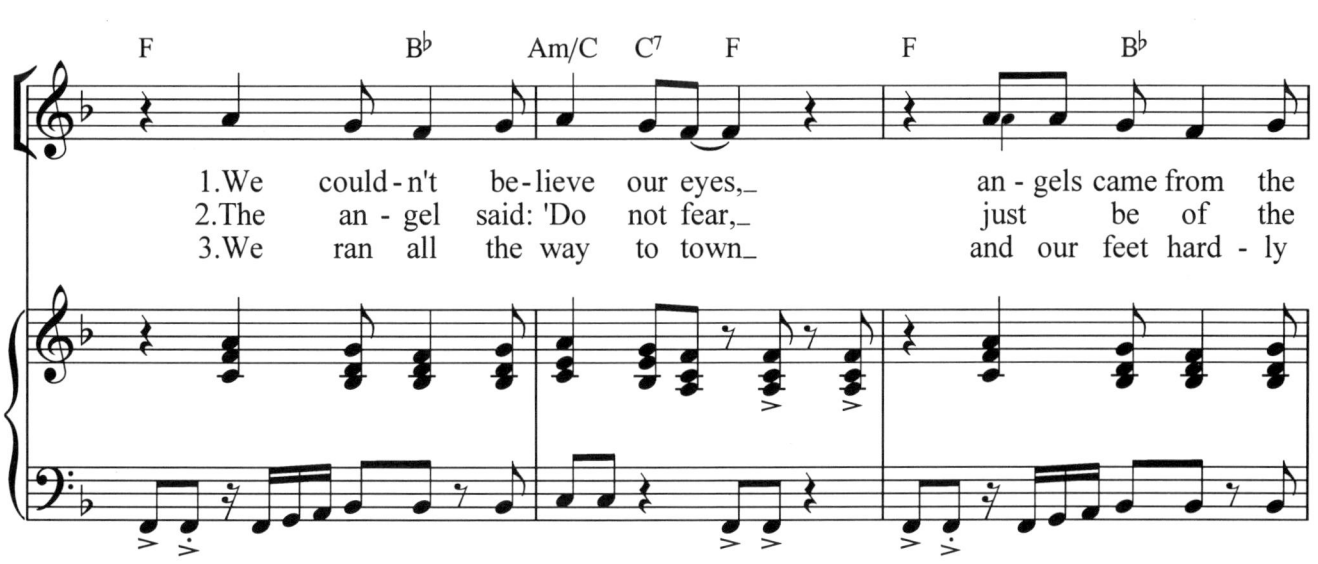

1. We could-n't be-lieve our eyes,___ an - gels came from the
2. The an - gel said: 'Do not fear,___ just be of the
3. We ran all the way to town___ and our feet hard - ly

Copyright © 2001 OUT OF THE ARK MUSIC

21

F/A F B♭ C9 F Dm
star - ry skies,_ sing - ing prais - es to God on high_ for the
great - est cheer;_ in a sta - ble not far from here_ is the
touched the ground;_ kept on run - ning un - til we found_ the

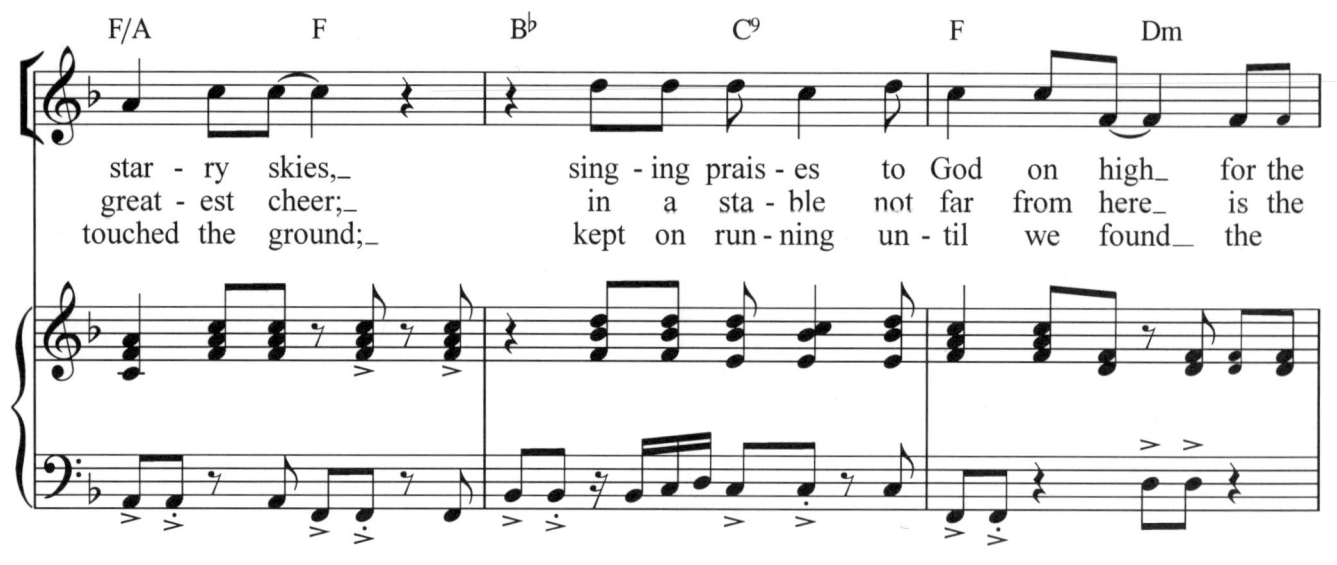

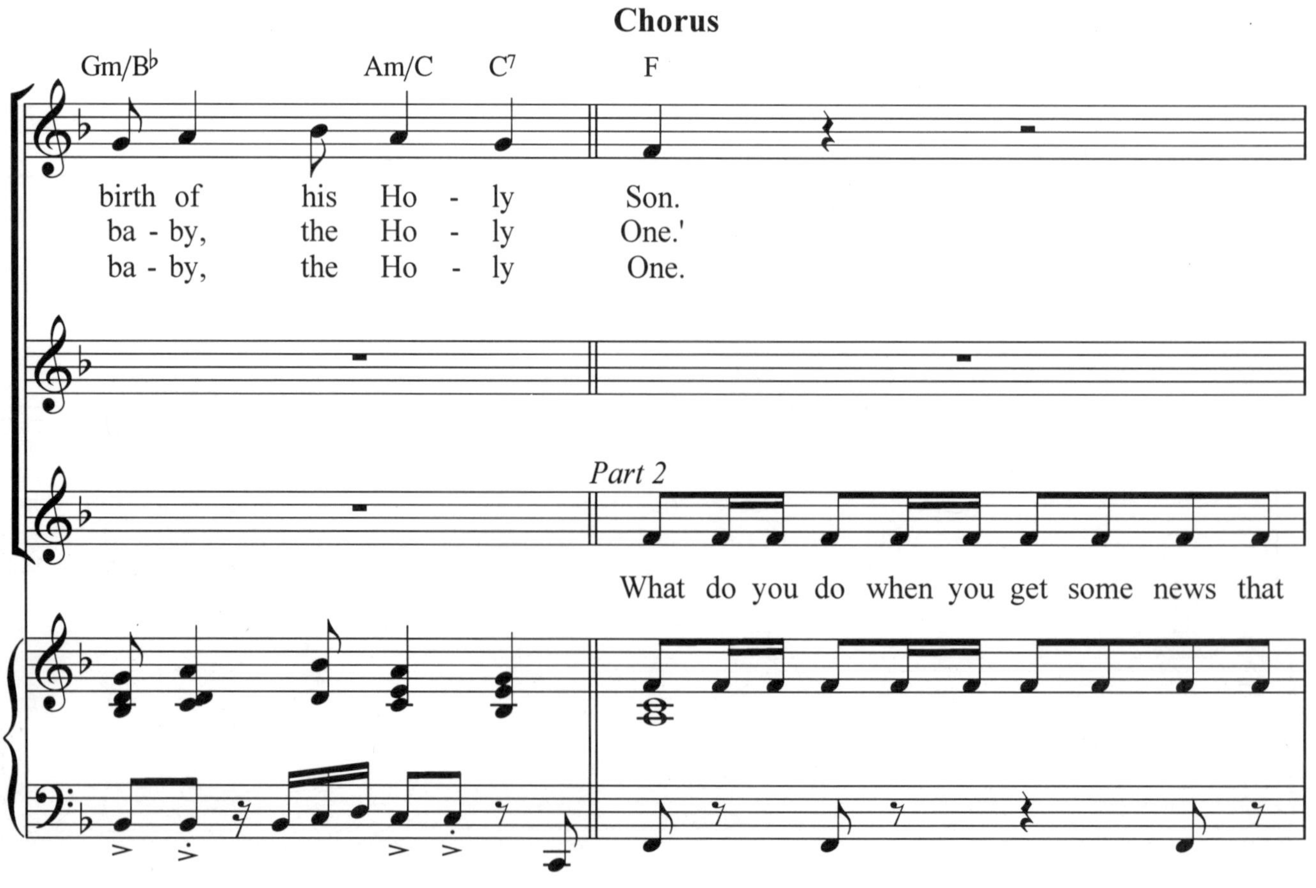
Chorus
Gm/B♭ Am/C C7 F
birth of his Ho - ly Son.
ba - by, the Ho - ly One.'
ba - by, the Ho - ly One.
Part 2
What do you do when you get some news that

ANGEL CONGA

Words and Music
MARGARET CARPENTER

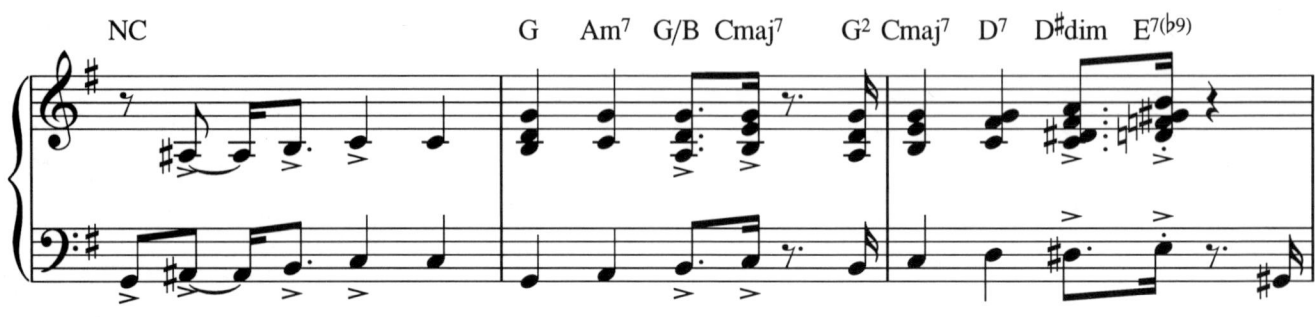

Copyright © 2001 OUT OF THE ARK MUSIC

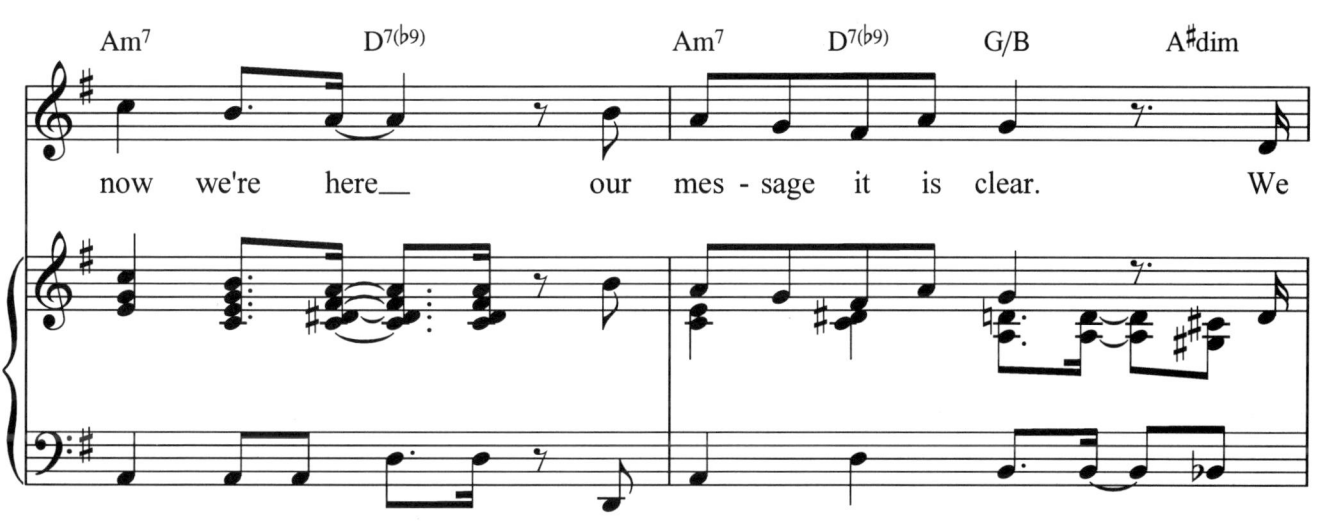
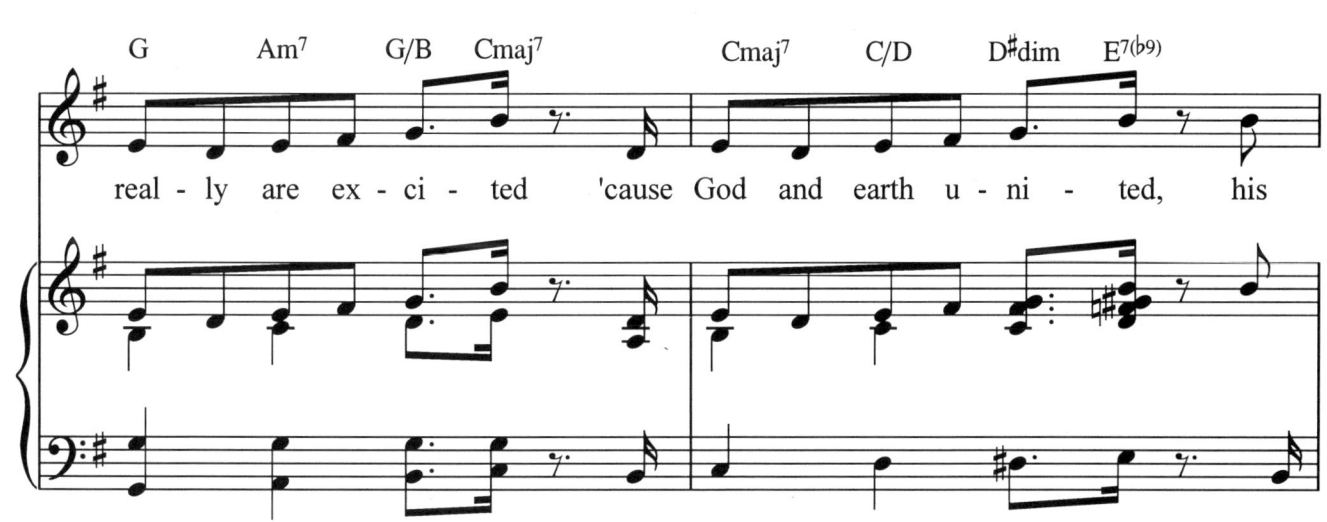

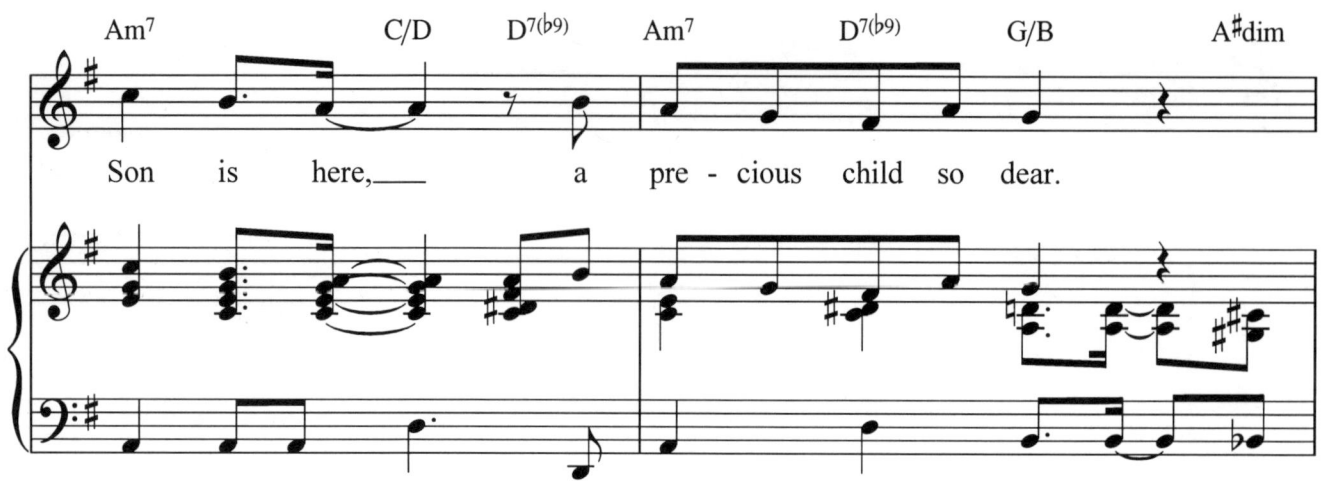

LISTEN TO THE NEWS

Words and Music
MARGARET CARPENTER

Copyright © 2001 OUT OF THE ARK MUSIC

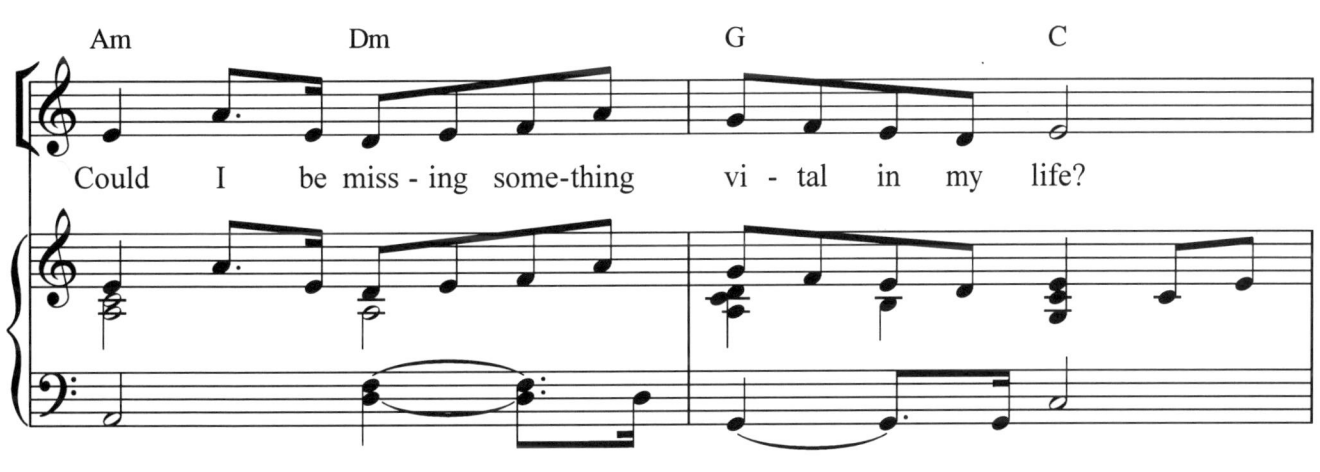

CHILDREN'S CAROL

Words and Music by
MARGARET CARPENTER

Copyright © 2001 OUT OF THE ARK MUSIC

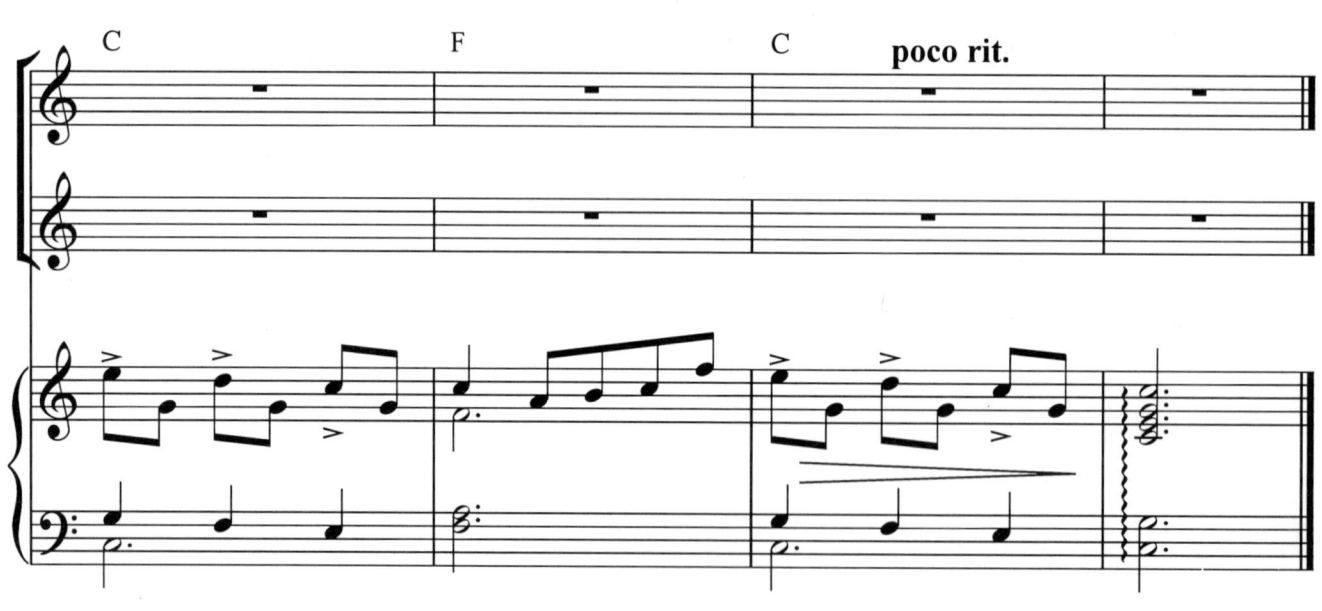

WISE MEN'S SONG

Words and Music
MARGARET CARPENTER

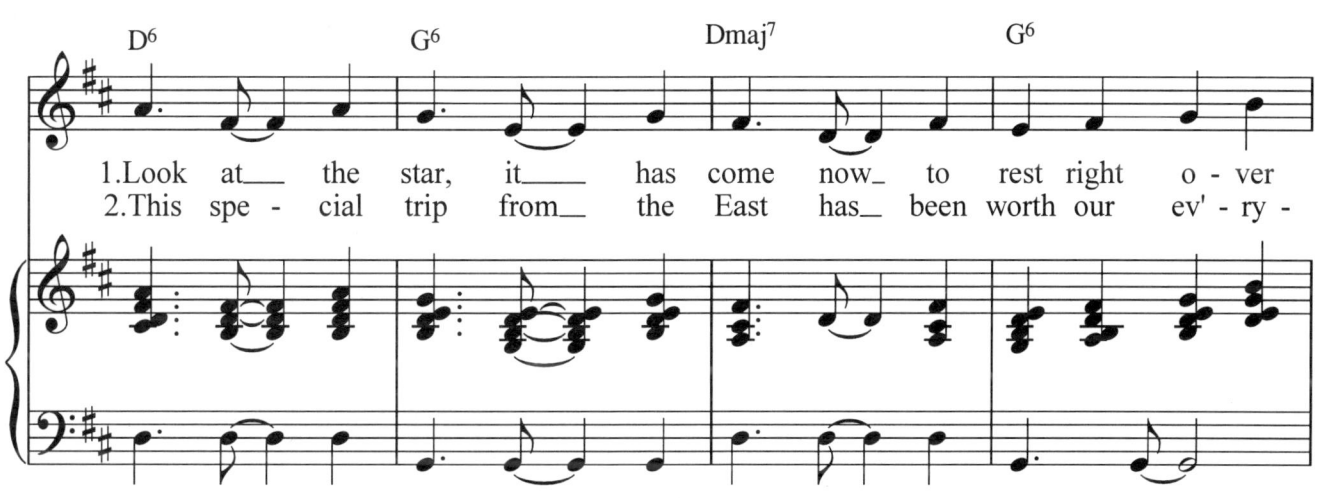

1. Look at the star, it has come now to rest right over
2. This special trip from the East has been worth our ev'ry-

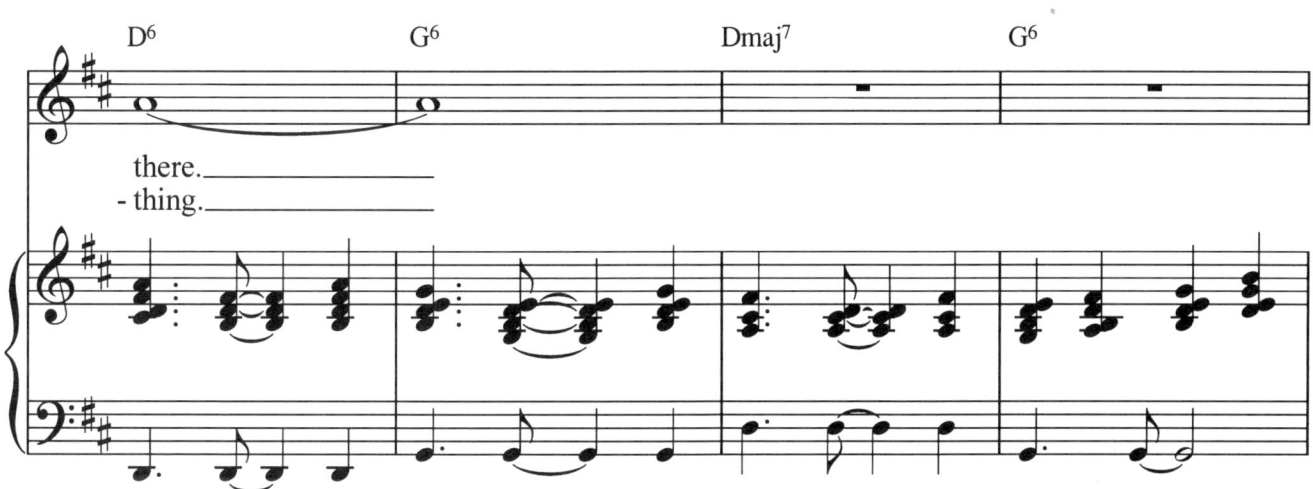

there.
-thing.

Copyright © 2001 OUT OF THE ARK MUSIC

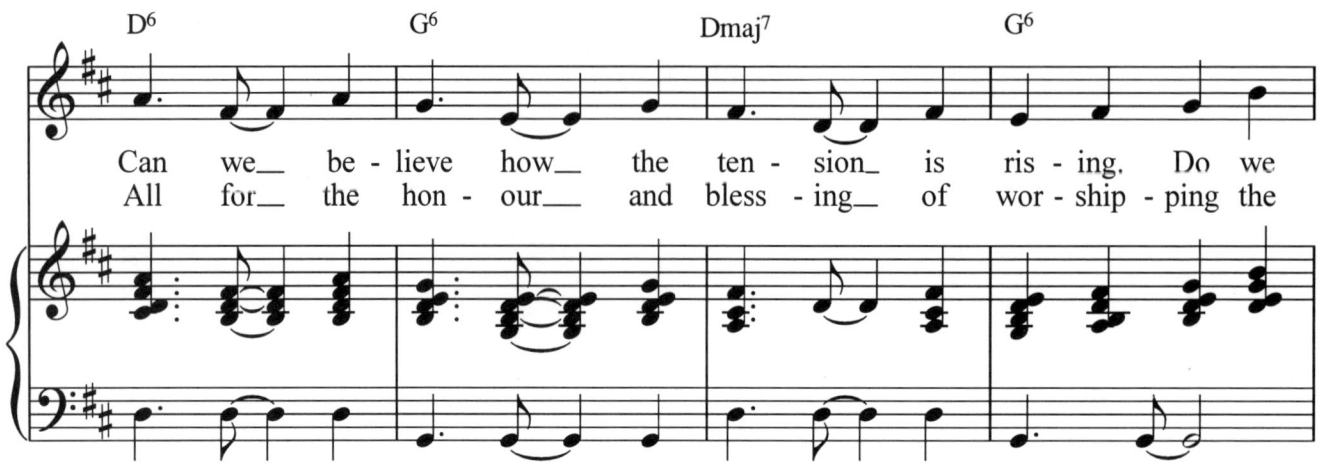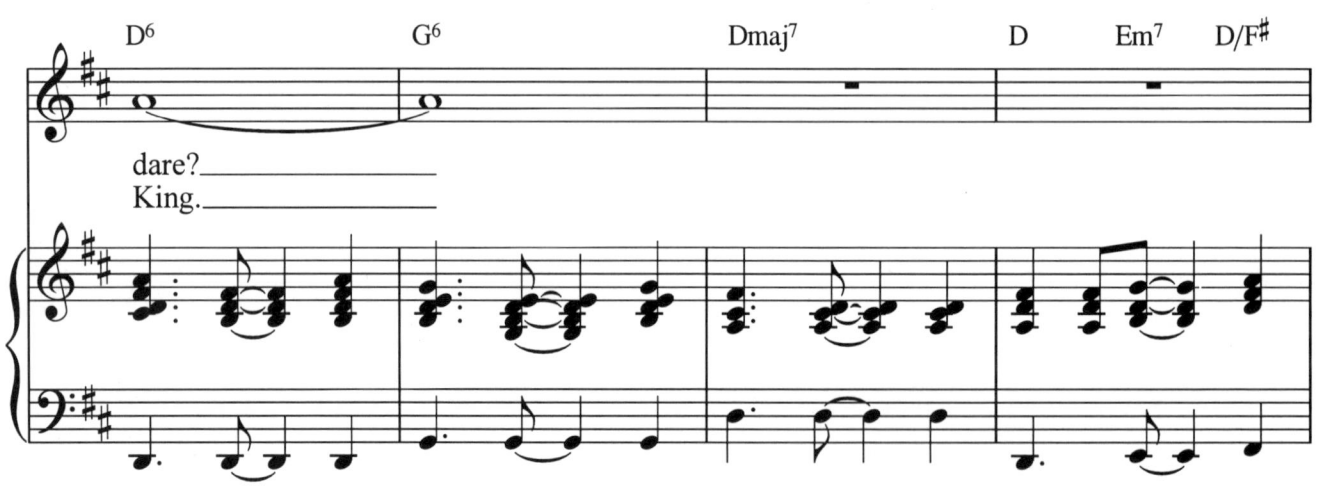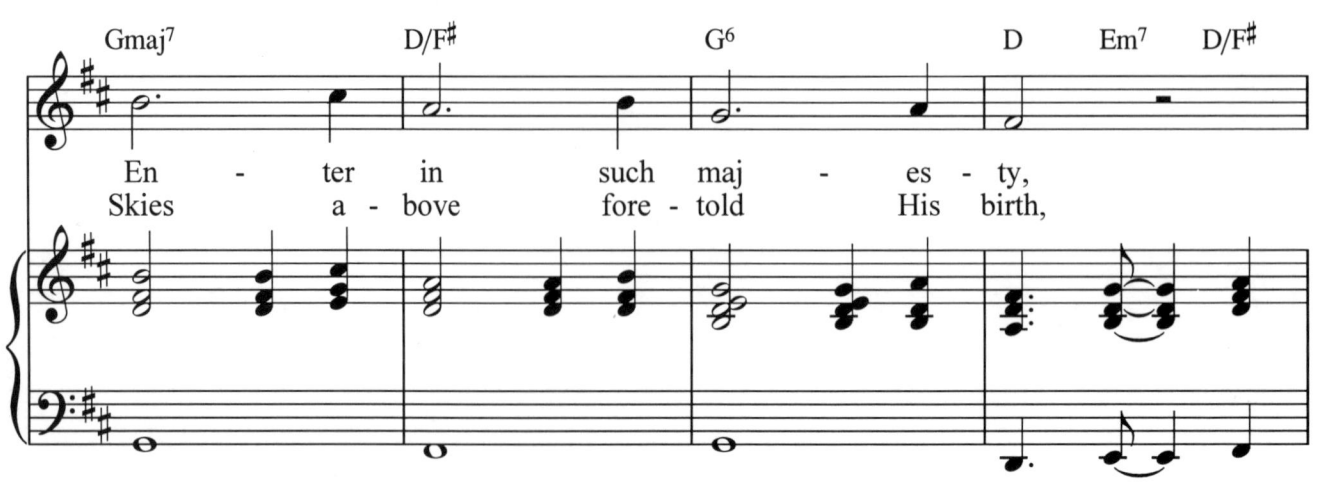

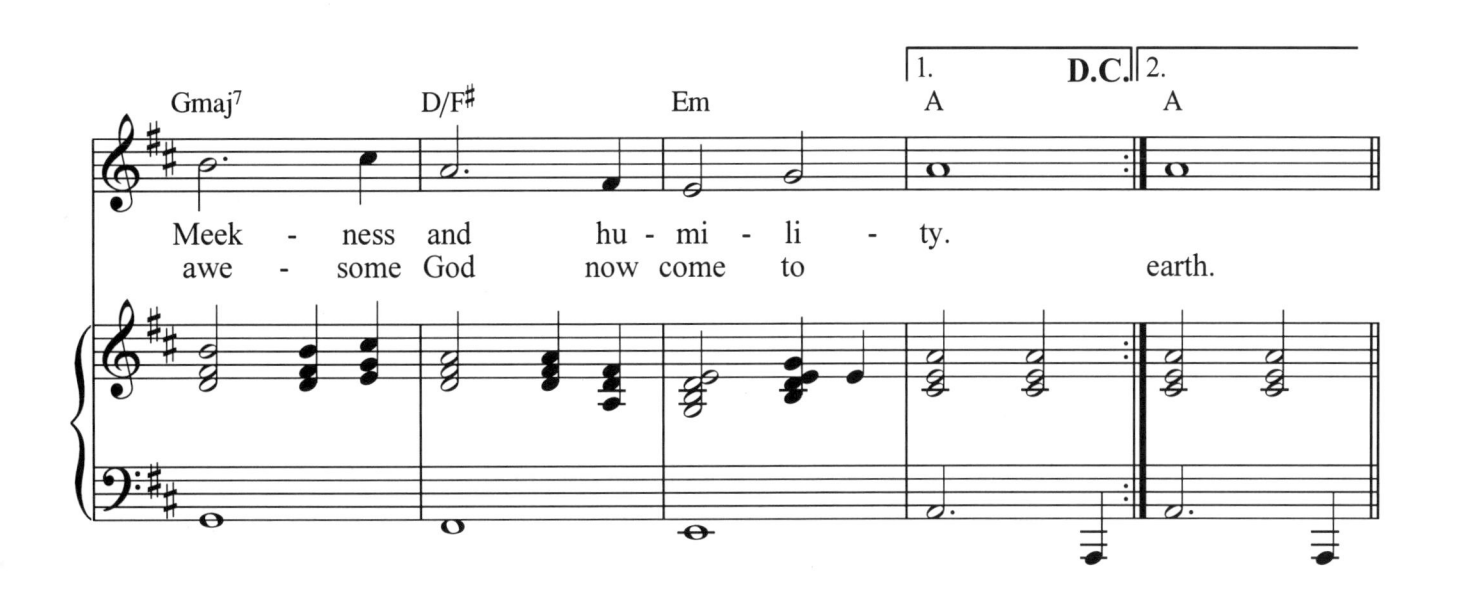

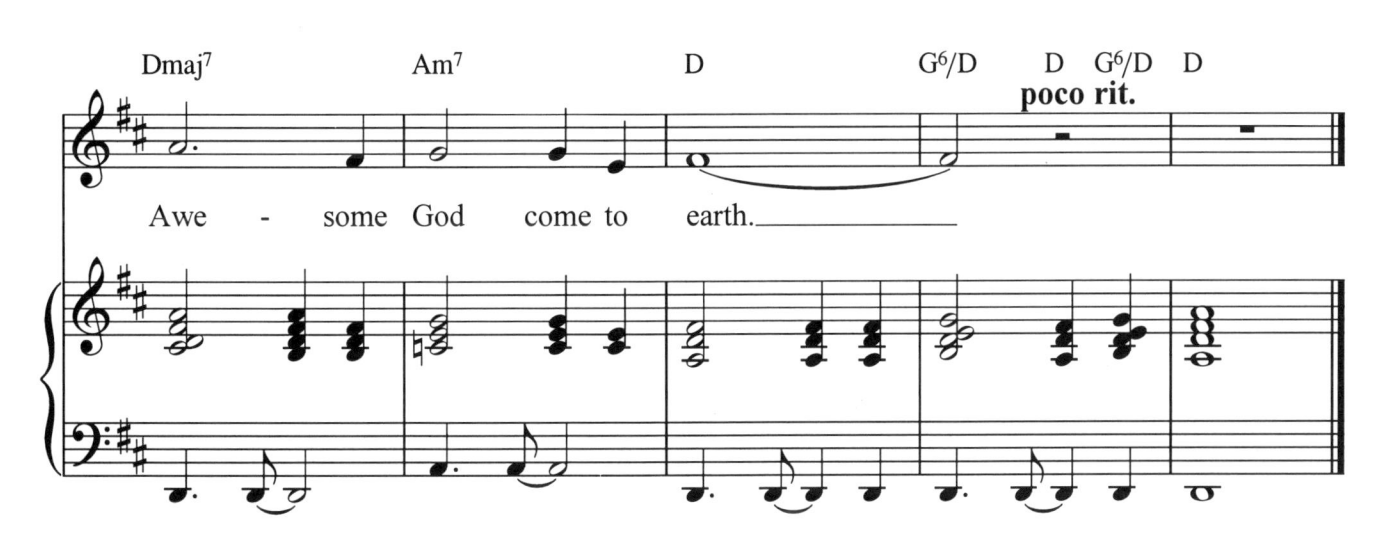

Meek - ness and hu - mi - li - ty.
awe - some God now come to earth.

Awe - some God come to earth.

Awe - some God come to earth.

poco rit.

THIS DAY

Words and music
MARGARET CARPENTER

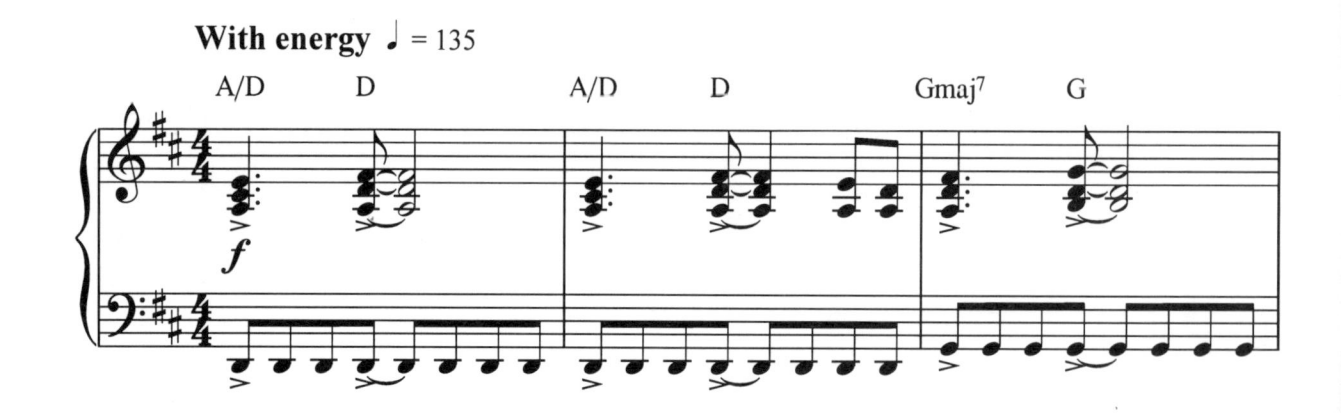

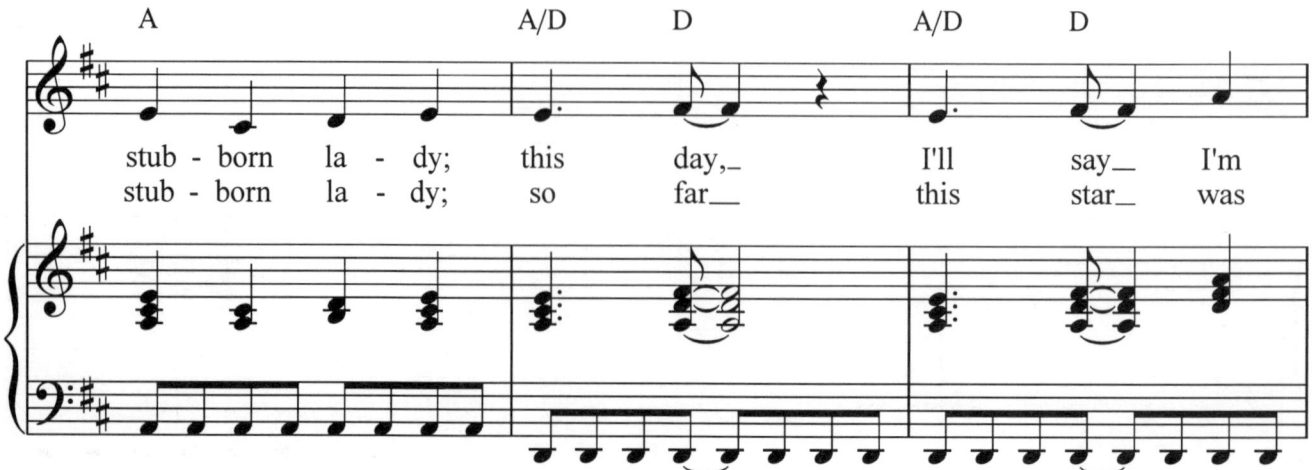

With energy ♩ = 135

1. This day,_ I'll say_ I've been such_ a stub-born la-dy; this day,_ I'll say_ I'm
2. You're right,_ this night_ I've been such_ a stub-born la-dy; so far_ this star_ was

Copyright © 2001 OUT OF THE ARK MUSIC

G(add 9) G Asus A G
sor - ry__ to all. Ev' - ry - one__ kept
there all__ a - long. I could ve - ry
F♯ Bm Em/G Gmaj7
tell - ing me__ this night was mak - ing his - to - ry.__ I'm
ea - si - ly__ have missed this night of mys - te - ry.__ I'm
Em9 Em A7 D
sor - ry,__ I've been a fool.
sor - ry,__ I've been so wrong.

Chorus

But now I'm here, let's have a party, let's celebrate in style. We've got the angels and the wise men, they'll be here for a while.

1. while.
2. while. This day I'll say I've

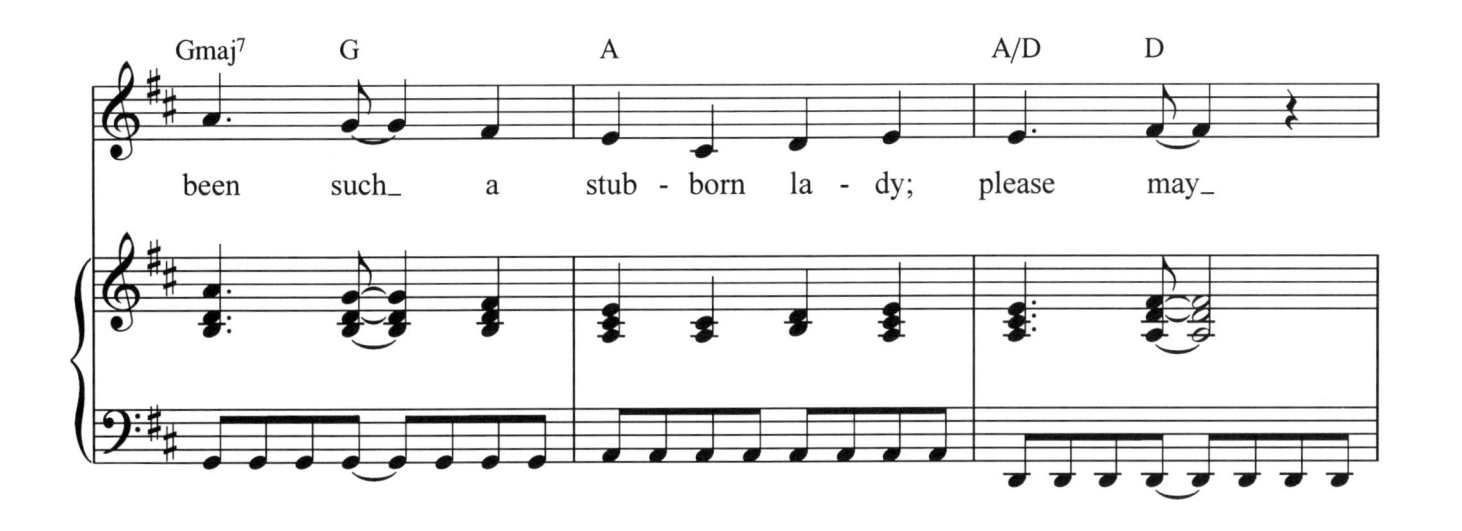

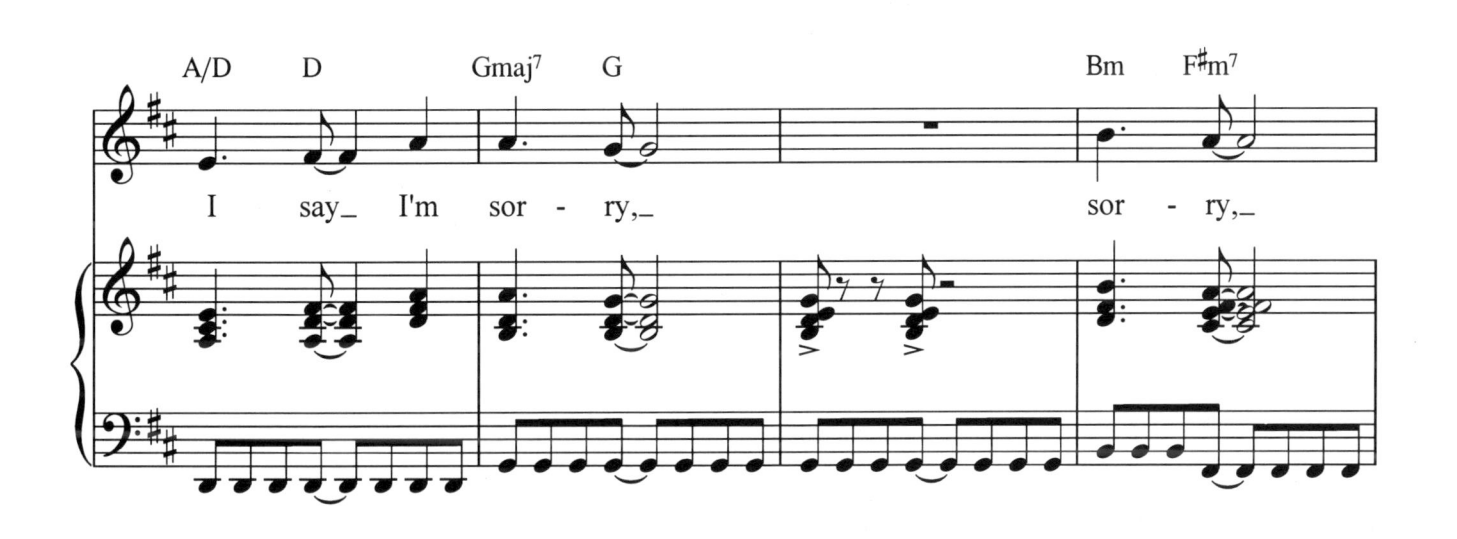

been such a stubborn lady; please may I say I'm sorry, sorry, Sorry to all.

BABOUSHKA

Words and Music
MARGARET CARPENTER

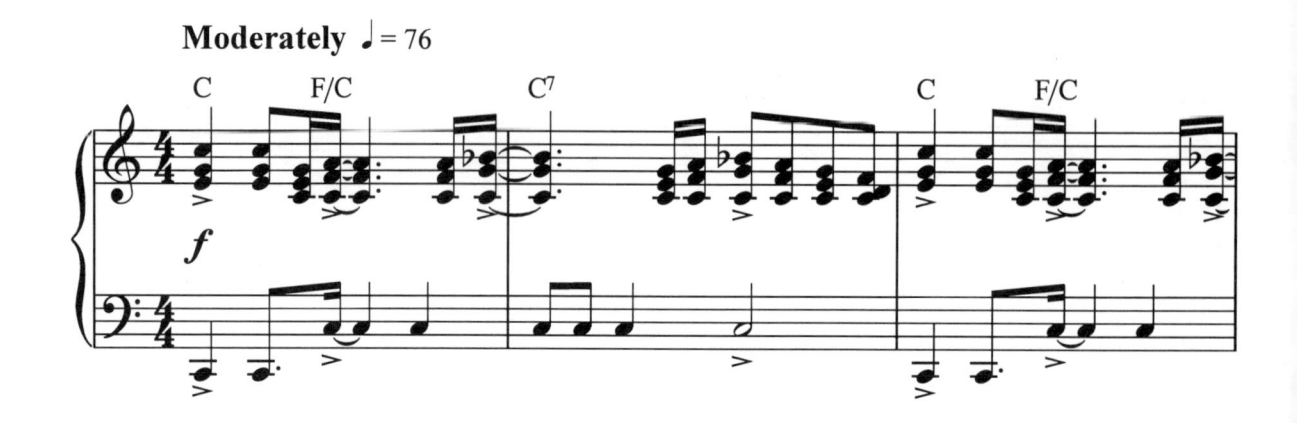

Moderately ♩ = 76

1. Now you've heard the story of Baboushka, how she very nearly missed the King;
2. Don't be unbelieving like Baboushka, you, this Christmas-time can be the one;
3. Don't be unbelieving like Baboushka, you, this Christmas-time can be the one;

Copyright © 2001 OUT OF THE ARK MUSIC

changed her mind in time, did dear Ba-boush-ka,
you can see this Je-sus like Ba-boush-ka,
you can see this Je-sus like Ba-boush-ka,

3rd time to Coda

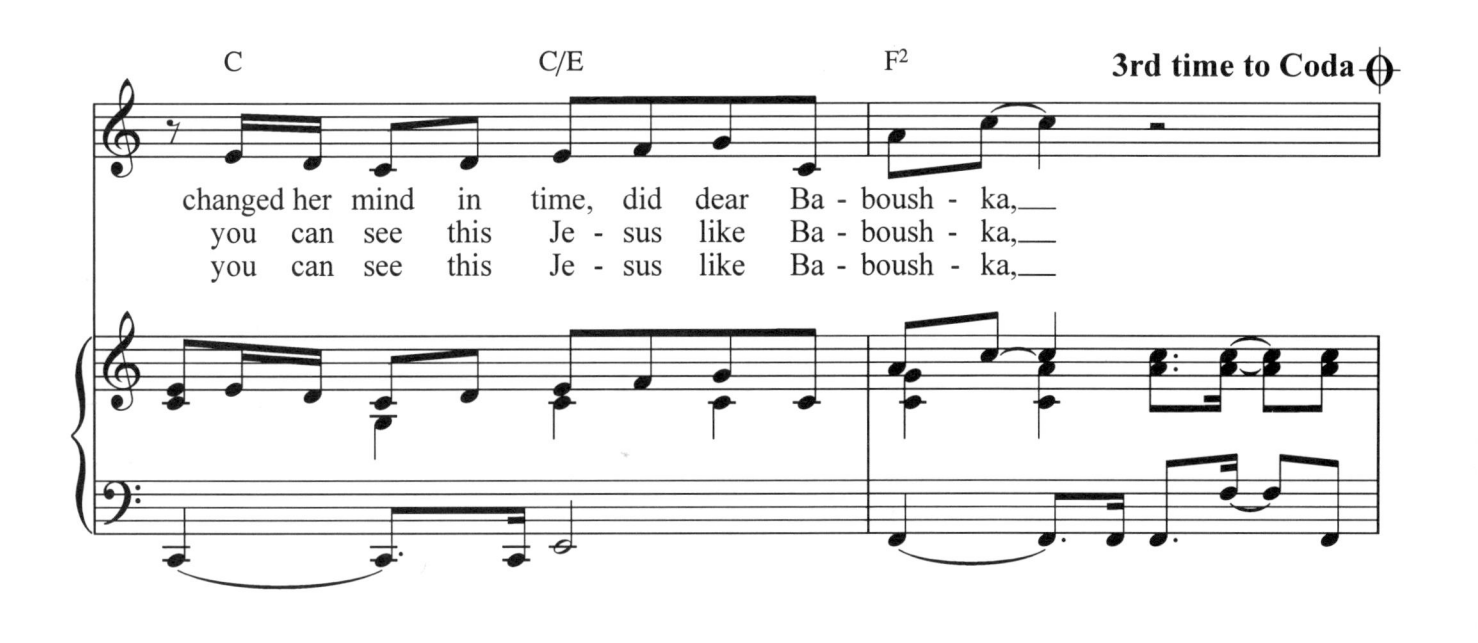

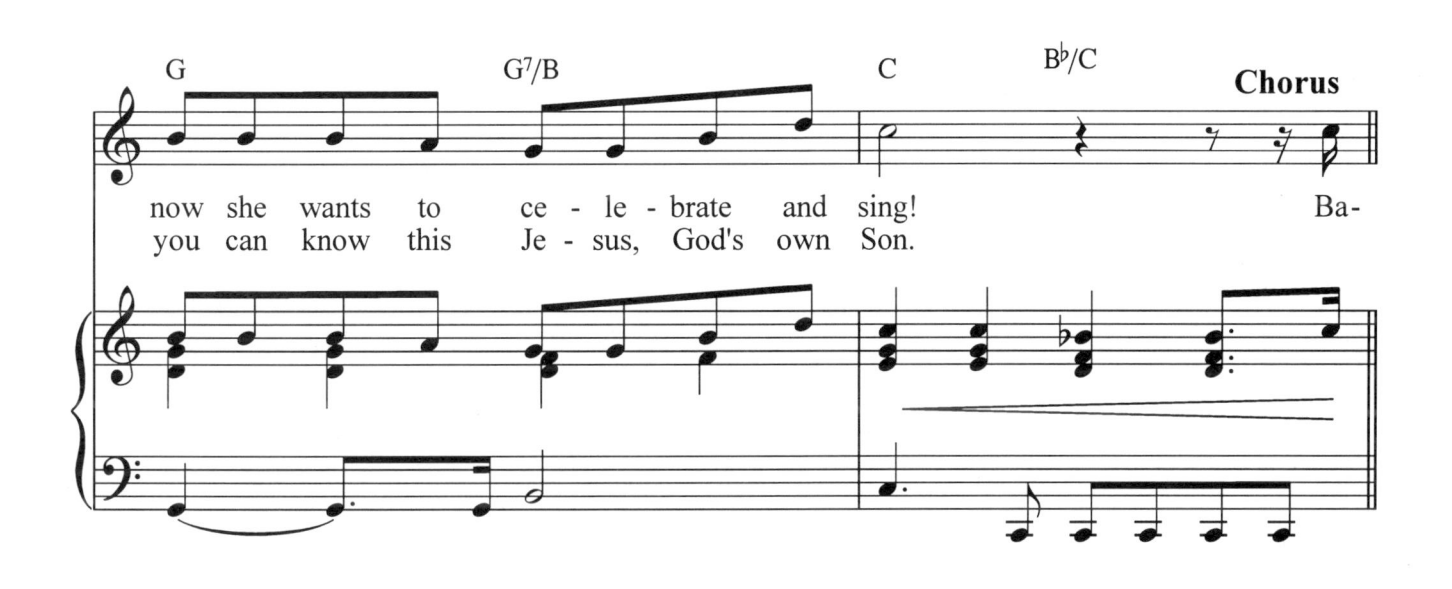

now she wants to ce-le-brate and sing! Ba-
you can know this Je-sus, God's own Son.

Chorus

-boush-ka, Ba-boush-ka, op-en wide your eyes and you will

C C7/E F C
see. Ba-boush-ka, Ba-boush-ka,
1. 2. al Coda
G G7/B C F/C C F/C
ba-by Je-sus came for you and me. me.
CODA
G7 G
you can know that he, do you know that he, you can know this

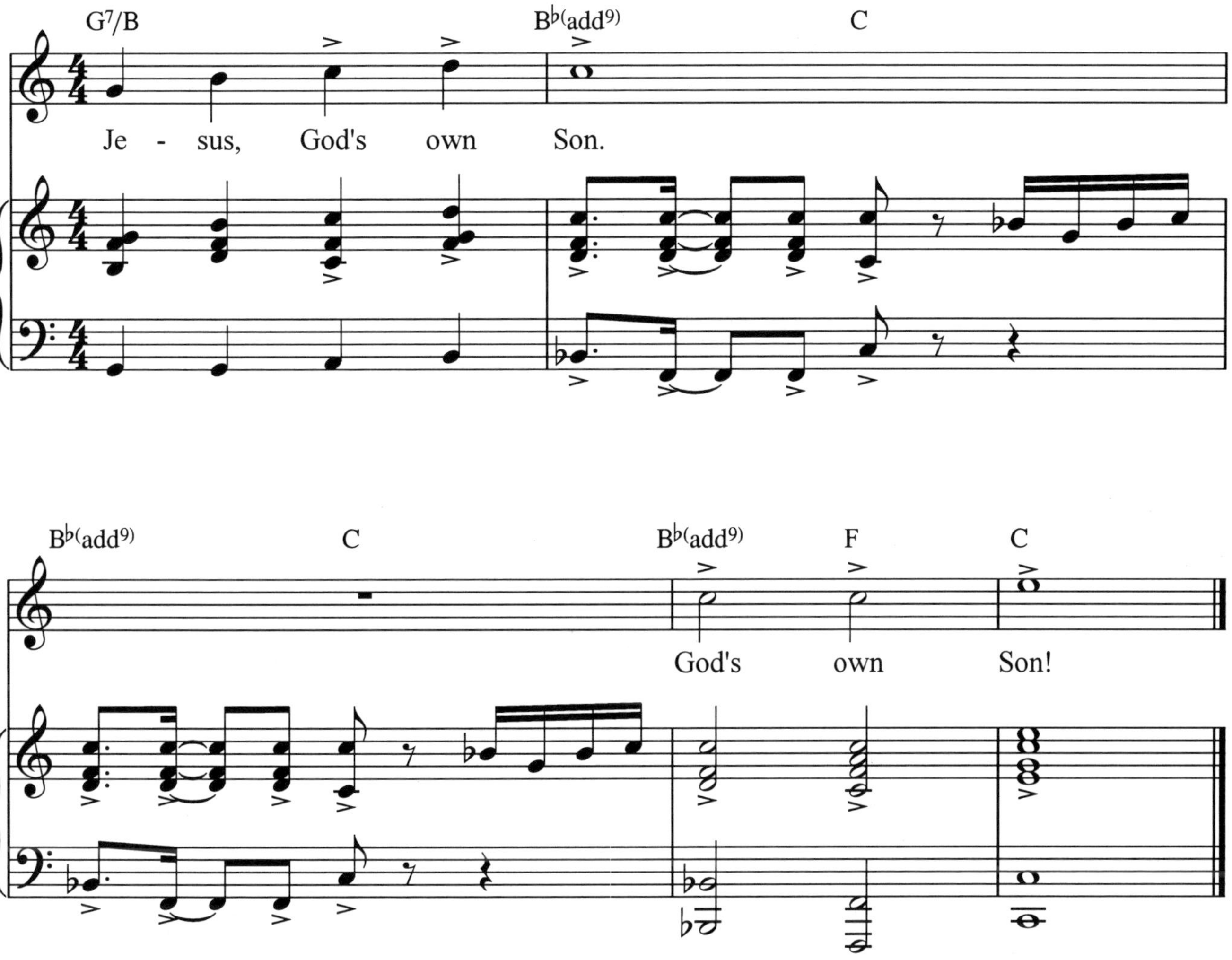
G7/B
B♭(add9)
C
Je - sus, God's own Son.
B♭(add9)
C
B♭(add9)
F
C
God's own Son!

HAVE YOU HEARD THE STORY?
(Song 1)

1   Have you heard the story of Baboushka?
         Heart of gold but stubborn to the last.
         Unbelieving, lovable Baboushka
         Nearly let the chance of a life-time pass.

CHORUS   *Baboushka, Baboushka,*
              Open wide your eyes and you will see.
              Baboushka, Baboushka,
              Baby Jesus came for you and me.

2   Listen carefully to how Baboushka
         Nearly let her stubborn heart turn cold.
         On that very special night Baboushka
         Heard the greatest story ever told.

         CHORUS

         Repeat CHORUS

© 2001 OUT OF THE ARK MUSIC

SONG OF THE TREES
(Song 2)

'Yoo,' whispered all the trees.
'Yoo,' sang the quiet breeze.
Listen to the news in the air tonight,
Look up to the sky, see the star so bright.

'Yoo,' whispered all the trees.
'Yoo,' sang the quiet breeze.
Listen to the news in the air tonight,
Look up to the sky, see the star so bright.
Listen, listen, listen to the wind tonight.

INSTRUMENTAL

Listen to the news in the air tonight,
Look up to the sky, see the star so bright.
Listen, listen, listen to the wind tonight.

© 2001 OUT OF THE ARK MUSIC

WHO'S THAT KNOCKING?
(Song 3)

1	Who's that knocking on my door,
Can I never get a moment's peace?
All night long just knock, knock, knock,
Will the callers never cease?
Lots of weary travellers
Keep mentioning the star,
But I've seen stars a million times before
So stop knocking on my door.

2	Who's that knocking on her door,
Can she never get a moment's peace?
All night long just knock, knock, knock,
Will the callers never cease?
Lots of weary travellers
Keep mentioning the star,
But she's seen stars a million times before
So stop knocking on her door.

Please stop, don't knock on the door!
YEAH!

© 2001 OUT OF THE ARK MUSIC

CHECK IT OUT!
(Song 4)

1   We couldn't believe our eyes,
　　Angels came from the starry skies,
　　Singing praises to God on high
　　For the birth of his Holy Son.

CHORUS

Part 2　　*What do you do when you get some news*
　　　　　　That lights your fuse, do you feel confused?
Parts 1 & 2　　*Just stay cool don't be a fool*
　　　　　　　And check it out, check it out!

2   The angel said: 'Do not fear,
　　Just be of the greatest cheer;
　　In a stable not far from here
　　Is the baby, the Holy One.'

　　　CHORUS

3   We ran all the way to town
　　And our feet hardly touched the ground;
　　Kept on running until we found
　　The baby, the Holy One.

CHORUS

Part 2　　*What do you do when you get some news*
　　　　　　That lights your fuse, do you feel confused?
Parts 1 & 2　　*Just stay cool don't be a fool*
　　　　　　　And dance and shout, dance and shout!

　　Check it out!

© 2001 OUT OF THE ARK MUSIC

ANGEL CONGA
(Song 5)

We're here to tell the story,
Came all the way from glory,
And now we're here
Our message it is clear.

We really are excited,
'Cause God and earth united,
His Son is here,
A precious child so dear.

CHORUS *Wonderful, wonderful love.*
Wonderful, marvellous joy.
Glorious news from the heav'ns above,
It's a baby, it's a baby boy!

We're here to tell the story,
Came all the way from glory,
And now we're here
Our message it is clear.

We really are excited,
'Cause God and earth united,
His Son is here,
A precious child so dear.

CHORUS

Share the good news,
Share the good news,
Share the good news,
Share the good news!

© 2001 OUT OF THE ARK MUSIC

LISTEN TO THE NEWS
(Song 6)

          Listen to the news.
          Listen to the news.

1   Ev'ry time I listen
          To the wind outside my door,
          I can hear it whisper
          That the news is good for sure.

CHORUS *Is there a message*
          In the air tonight?
          Could I be missing something
          Vital in my life?

Part 1	Part 2
Listen to the news	*Is there a message*
In the air tonight.	*In the air tonight?*
You could miss the most amazing	*Could I be missing something*
Night of your life.	*Vital in my life?*

2   All these people calling
          Do they know some mystery?
          Maybe heard the message
          That the wind is telling me.

          CHORUS

Listen to the news.	
Listen to the news.	
Listen to the news.	Listen,
Listen to the news.	Listen,
Listen to the news.	Listen,
Listen to the news.	Listen,
Listen to the news.	Listen,
Listen to the news.	To the news.

© 2001 OUT OF THE ARK MUSIC

THE CHILDREN'S CAROL
(Song 7)

Jesus, we're very glad
We made it to this place.
It has been worth it all
To look upon your face.
Tiny baby in the hay,
The angels sang about your birth,
Telling us the greatest news
'Hope for all the earth'.

Part 1
Jesus, we're very glad
We made it to this place.
It has been worth it all
To look upon your face.
Tiny baby in the hay,
The angels sang about your birth,
Telling us the greatest news
'Hope for all the earth'.

Part 2
Jesus,
Promised king.
Jesus,
To you we sing.
Jesus,
Your special birth was such
Good news and
'Hope for the earth'.

© 2001 OUT OF THE ARK MUSIC

WISE MEN'S SONG
(Song 8)

1   Look at the star it has come now
     To rest right over there.
     Can we believe how the tension
     Is rising. Do we dare?
     Enter in such majesty,
     Meekness and humility.

2   This special trip from the East has
     Been worth our ev'rything.
     All for the honour and blessing
     Of worshipping the King.
     Skies above foretold His birth,
     Awesome God now come to earth.

     Awesome God come to earth.
     Awesome God come to earth.

© 2001 OUT OF THE ARK MUSIC

THIS DAY
(Song 9)

1   This day, I'll say
          I've been such a stubborn lady;
          This day, I'll say
          I'm sorry to all.
          Ev'ryone kept telling me
          This night was making history
          I'm sorry, I've been a fool.

CHORUS   *But now I'm here, let's have a party,*
               Let's celebrate in style.
               We've got the angels and the wise men,
               They'll be here for a while.

2   You're right, this night
          I've been such a stubborn lady;
          So far, this star
          Was there all along.
          I could very easily
          Have missed this night of mystery,
          I'm sorry, I've been so wrong.

          CHORUS

          This day, I'll say
          I've been such a stubborn lady;
          Please may I say
          I'm sorry, sorry,
          Sorry to all.

© 2001 OUT OF THE ARK MUSIC

BABOUSHKA
(Song 10)

1 Now you've heard the story of Baboushka,
How she very nearly missed the King;
Changed her mind in time, did dear Baboushka,
Now she wants to celebrate and sing!

CHORUS *Baboushka, Baboushka,*
Open wide your eyes and you will see.
Baboushka, Baboushka,
Baby Jesus came for you and me.

2 Don't be unbelieving like Baboushka,
You, this Christmas-time can be the one;
You can see this Jesus like Baboushka,
You can know this Jesus, God's own son.

CHORUS

3 Don't be unbelieving like Baboushka,
You, this Christmas-time can be the one;
You can see this Jesus like Baboushka,
You can know that he, do you know that he,
You can know this Jesus, God's own Son.
God's own Son!

© 2001 OUT OF THE ARK MUSIC

LICENCE APPLICATION FORM

Should you decide to stage this musical, you will need to photocopy and fill in the form below and return it to the publishers, in order to apply for a licence. Licences start from as little as £10 + VAT, depending on your requirements.

APPLICATION FOR A LICENCE

To: **OUT OF THE ARK MUSIC**
Sefton House
2 Molesey Road
Hersham Green, Walton-On Thames
Surrey, KT12 4RQ

Fax: (01932) 703010

We wish to stage	"BABOUSHKA" by Margaret Carpenter
At (name of school/theatre group)	
On (dates of production)	
Number of public performances	
Total seating capacity of venue	
Expected audience size per performance (excluding pupils)	
Will words to songs be provided in programmes?	
Will admission be charged?	
If so, please give details of ticket prices	
Name of organiser/producer	
Address of school/theatre group Postcode	
Daytime telephone number	
Are you recording the show?	
Sound recording YES/NO	No. of recordings/copies
Video recording YES/NO	No. of recordings/copies